"A German shepherd is the quintessential dog."
—Mordecai Siegal and Matthew Margolis, *The Good Shepherd*, 1996

Love of German Shepherds

The Ultimate Tribute

Todd R. Berger, Editor

Voyageur Press

PetLife
LIBRARY

Dedication

To Mom, Taj, Johann, and Max

Compiled and edited by Todd R. Berger
Designed by Andrea Rud
Printed in Hong Kong

99   00   01   02   03   5   4   3   2   1

Library of Congress Cataloging-in-Publication Data
  Love of German shepherds : the ultimate tribute / Todd
  R. Berger, editor.
      p.   cm. — (Petlife library)
  ISBN 0-89658-446-1
  1. German shepherd dog—Anecdotes. I. Berger,
  Todd R., 1968–   . II. Series.
  SF429.G37L68   1999
  636.737'6—dc21   99–13245
                                              CIP

Distributed in Canada by Raincoast Books
8680 Cambie Street, Vancouver, B.C. V6P 6M9

Published by Voyageur Press, Inc.
123 North Second Street, P.O. Box 338
Stillwater, MN 55082 U.S.A.
651-430-2210, fax 651-430-2211

Permissions

We have made every effort to determine original sources and locate copyright holders of the excerpts in this book. Grateful acknowledgment is made to the writers, publishers, and agencies listed below for permission to reprint material copyrighted or controlled by them. Please bring to our attention any errors of fact, omission, or copyright.

"Amigo" from *Where the Grass Is Greener and Dogs Had Better Keep Off* by Ora Spaid. Copyright © 1995 by Ora Spaid. Reprinted by permission of the author.

"The Two Tulips" from *My Dog Tulip* by J.R. Ackerley. Copyright © 1965 by J.R. Ackerley. Copyright renewed 1998 by Francis King. Reprinted by permission of Harold Ober Associates Incorporated.

"The Dog With a Hollow Leg" by Ken W. Purdy. Copyright © 1961 by Curtis Publishing Corp. Originally appeared in *The Saturday Evening Post* for July 8, 1961. Reprinted by permission of the author's estate and its agents, Scott Meredith Literary Agency L.P.

"The Phantom Car Gang" from *My Dog Rex* by Arthur Holman. Copyright © 1957 by Arthur Holman. Reprinted by permission of Eric Dobby Publishing Ltd.

"First Lady of the Seeing Eye" by Morris Frank and Blake Clark. Copyright © 1957 by Morris Frank and Blake Clark. Reprinted by permission of The Seeing Eye.

Section I of "The Angry Winter" from *The Unexpected Universe* by Loren Eiseley. Copyright © 1968 by Loren Eiseley and renewed 1996 by John A. Eichman III. Reprinted by permission of Harcourt Brace & Company.

Page 1: *A trio of German shepherd pups. (Photograph © Alan and Sandy Carey)*

Page 2–3: *The unmistakable outline of a shepherd at sunset in Yellowstone National Park. (Photograph © Jeff and Alexa Henry)*

Page 3, inset: *With patient eyes, a German shepherd waits for its owner on a summer beach. (Photograph © Roxanne Kjarum)*

Facing page: *The German shepherd is perhaps the most loyal breed, a dog that will bond with you tightly and always wish to be by your side. (Photograph © Jeff and Alexa Henry)*

Page 6: *A shepherd lounges along a northern trail. (Photograph © Roxanne Kjarum)*

Contents

Introduction

by Todd R. Berger

 Friend or foe? For many, this is the question that arises when crossing paths with a German shepherd. Some might say "foe," perhaps out of fear of this strong, intelligent, and fiercely loyal breed. But most who truly know German shepherds will unequivocally say "friend." Many of the traits that lead some to fear the breed are the very reasons people who truly know German shepherds love them. This book is for people who love German shepherds like I do.

Love of German Shepherds is an unabashedly pro–German shepherd celebration. After all, with German shepherds, there's a lot to get excited about.

First of all, German shepherd pups are adorable. Those oversize feet, that goofy furball look, and haphazard ears that simply refuse to stand up straight are the definition of cute. All puppies are cute, but they're not German shepherd cute.

Not to be outdone, adult German shepherds are positively gorgeous. That noble head, those erect ears, a sleek, wolfish coat, a muscular chest, and a sloping body—quite frankly, this is the perfect dog.

But the German shepherd isn't just a pretty dog, it is also supremely intelligent. The reason German shepherds are used for so many different tasks—from herding sheep to assisting blind people to apprehending criminals to searching the ruins of bombed-out buildings—is that they are smart enough to handle just about any job for which they are trained.

A German shepherd, with its noble head, beautiful coat, and radiating self-confidence, is a stunningly beautiful dog. (Photograph © Sharon Eide/Elizabeth Flynn)

However, if the only traits that attracted people to German shepherds were good looks and keen intelligence, I suggest the relationship would be somewhat superficial. There's another ingredient: loyalty. You are the world to your shepherd, and she will do anything for you. For almost all German shepherd owners, the feeling is mutual.

A Brief History of the German Shepherd Dog

Like the words "gin and tonic" to a bartender, a lot of information is gleaned from the breed name "German shepherd." An inexperienced bartender might have to consult a drink guide to prepare a Manhattan, just as your average person would have to consult a breed guide to learn about the origins of the beagle. To make a long story short, the German shepherd originated in Germany as a sheep-herding dog—though the later history of the breed drifted far from its woolly foundation.

Sheep herders in Germany used a variety of "German sheep dogs" over the centuries to fill the essential role of protecting the flock from predators, of keeping the flock together to avoid this or that sheep from straying too far afield, and of moving sheep to market. These dogs were not of a consistent breed type—some had wavy coats while others were smooth-coats; some were black and tan while others were black and white; and some had retriever-like drooped ears while others had shepherd-style erect ears.

Toward the end of the nineteenth century, interest in dog shows grew in Europe, thus interest grew in Germany to develop a breed standard for these diverse types of German sheep dogs. A German cavalry officer, Captain Max von Stephanitz, decided to do something about it.

In 1899, von Stephanitz and two others founded the Verein für deutsche Schäferhunde (SV), the second club to be formed around the goal of standardizing the German sheep dogs. (The first, known as the Phylax Society, survived only three years in the early 1890s.) Starting the year it was founded, the SV sponsored *Sieger* Shows to choose a *Sieger* and *Siegerin* (male and female national champions) of the breed. As judge, von Stephanitz was able to control the development of the breed, for most breeders wanted to breed their bitches to the reigning champion. Von Stephanitz chose dogs closest to his ideals for the breed and avoided dogs that exhibited undesirable characteristics; the dogs he chose were the least likely to pass any negative traits to their offspring. In describing a dog named Horand v Grafrath, the captain's model for the breed and the first dog registered with the SV, von Stephanitz articulated his ideals for the breed: It should have "powerful bones, beautiful lines, and a nobly formed head" and possess "the straightforward nature of a gentleman with a boundless and irrepressible zest for living." He went on to say the breed would be by nature obedient to its master and "never idle, always on the go; well disposed to harmless people, but no cringer, crazy about children, and always in love." Sound familiar? We who love German shepherds today owe it all to Captain

Facing page: *The highly intelligent German shepherd is used for a wide variety of tasks; this search-and-rescue dog assists rangers with the U.S. National Park Service. (Photograph © Jeff and Alexa Henry)*

Max von Stephanitz, who stuck to those ideals and oversaw the development of the German shepherd for thirty-four years as president of the SV.

Von Stephanitz also saw the utilitarian value of the breed, and he appealed to police organizations to make use of the German shepherd. Indeed, after the turn of the century, police units all over Germany adopted the dogs to train for police work. During the First World War, the military also brought the German shepherd into service as guard dog, Red Cross dog, and as messenger. These dogs on the German frontlines caught the attention of the Americans and the British, and, soon after the end of the war, the United States, Great Britain, Canada, and many other countries began to import the German shepherd in large numbers. Shortly thereafter, breeders went to work around the world.

One of the most interesting stories regarding the German shepherd breed unfolded in Great Britain after the First World War—and continued until relatively recently. From the British point of view of the day, it wasn't exactly fashionable to begin importing and breeding a new kind of dog with the name "German" shepherd. Consequently, the British renamed the breed the Alsatian Wolf Dog, as some of the dogs had come from Alsace-Lorraine along the French-German border, and as the dogs looked like wolves. In 1936, the wolf moniker was dropped and the name "Alsatian (German Shepherd Dog)" became the official name of the breed in England. It wasn't until the 1970s that The Kennel Club of Great Britain began to seriously discuss changing the official name of the breed to German Shepherd Dog, which is the literal translation of the German *deutscher Schäferhund*—a name (in translation) the rest of the world had adopted decades earlier. In 1977, a motion to change the name was approved, and, although the dog is still called the Alsatian in some official circles, that name is becoming less and less common in the UK.

In the 1920s, the German shepherd exploded in popularity around the world, as this lovable, utilitarian, beautiful dog caught the heart of everyone from police organizations to dog show breeders, from soldiers to families. In addition, as you will read about in "First Lady of the Seeing Eye," trainers in Germany and Switzerland began to train German shepherds as guide dogs for the blind. A dog that did not exist as a breed a quarter century earlier now seemed like a dog the world could not live without. Today, the German shepherd is one of the most popular dogs in the world, used by a wide variety of organizations and loved by thousands of families.

About *Love of German Shepherds*

Love of German Shepherds is a first-of-its-kind tribute to the breed, collecting wonderful stories and beautiful photographs to try to get close to the heart of why so many people love German shepherds so much. The diverse writers whose stories make up this book come from a variety of backgrounds: Arthur Holman was a police dog trainer;

An adolescent pup with a tongue as long as its snout gets a hug. (Photograph © David H. Smith)

Morris Frank was the blind founder of the Seeing Eye, Inc.; Julie Campbell was a popular author of stories for adolescent girls; Loren Eiseley was an anthropologist. What unites these writers is, first of all, good writing. They have diverse voices, but all have extraordinary talent. Secondly, they all write of a love for German shepherds, whether the dogs were their own pets or characters in a well-spun tale.

In addition to the literary talent displayed, *Love of German Shepherds* is also a visual feast. Here you will see the work of exceptional photographers, who also carry us a little closer to the nature of the German shepherd. In these pages, you will see the work of Frank S. Balthis, Norvia Behling, Alan and Sandy Carey, David F. Clobes, Kent and Donna Dannen, Tara Darling, Sharon Eide and Elizabeth Flynn, Jeff and Alexa Henry, Roxanne Kjarum, Anne Mannik, Phil Marques, William H. Mullins, David H. Smith, Kelly Vickery, Barbara von Hoffmann, and Marilyn "Angel" Wynn.

Enough said; it's time to begin. Sit back and enjoy *Love of German Shepherds*—preferably with a big ole pointy-eared head laying in your lap.

A foursome of puppies with heaps of "German shepherd cuteness." (Photograph © Isabelle Francais)

PART I

A Powerful Bond

"As we drove out of the yard I looked back on a sight I will always remember. The master had started down a lane with a wheelbarrow, his tall spare figure outlined against the landscape, and ahead of him, back of him and at his side about a dozen dogs, tails waving, eyes eager, glorying in this companionship with the one they worshiped. A picture depicting in all its vividness the true setting for a Shepherd, man's constant companion."
—W. J. Hickmott, Jr., *Paw Marks*, 1932

Above: *German shepherds and children bond when the dog is but a pup, and the bond lasts a canine lifetime. (Photograph © Kent and Donna Dannen)*

Left: *The German shepherd's loyal and protective nature lead shepherds to bond very closely to their owners. (Photograph © Frank S. Balthis)*

Amigo

by Ora Spaid

 German shepherds—perhaps due to their intelligence, perhaps due to their fierce loyalty—bond intensely with their owners. But such bonding takes time, especially with a shepherd that finds its way to a home after puppyhood.

Ora Spaid opened his home to such a dog—an unwanted purebred—making room in his small apartment and busy life for the shepherd. But after all, it was love at first sight. As Spaid wrote: "Amigo was a sudden black presence moving excitedly from one of us to the other, tail aswish. A magnificent creature!" Spaid was smitten. Though Amigo proved more cautious in her affections, Spaid's story wonderfully illustrates the development of the unique bond between a person and a German shepherd.

Spaid is a former journalist and author of management training books. "Amigo" first appeared in Spaid's self-published book *Where the Grass Is Greener and the Dogs Had Better Keep Off* (1995).

❧

A shepherd on a late summer day in the Rocky Mountains. (Photograph © Jeff and Alexa Henry)

1

A LANDLADY WHO lets a tenant have a dog is tolerant. One who wants a renter to have a dog is rare. But a landlady who insists you have a dog, and sets about getting you one, is a pearl of great price.

Mary was such a jewel. Soon after I settled into my new apartment in Madison, she began hinting. First: "You really need a dog." Then: "A dog would add a lot to your life." Finally the hard sell: "You could do a lot for some dog who needs a home."

She was not intrusive, but from the first day it was evident she would be no repetition of those absentee urban landlords I never heard from as long as the rent was paid on time. Here I would be more than mere tenant, would be cared about, maybe even cared for. Before I moved in Mary and Georgia, the widow and part owner who occupied the front apartment, had given my empty place a woman's touch—drapes and curtains neatly shaped and a cot, blankets, table and chairs for use until my furniture arrived. Because I couldn't cook, I was often invited to dinner.

That first summer I was drawn into a convivial ritual at Mary's house called "porch time," a quieter, sit-down variation on the happy hour practiced elsewhere. Each weekday evening at 5, Mary holds court on her outside porch overlooking the river. Standing invitations go out in the spring with Mary's vernal greeting cards. She's a single woman in mid-life with few kin; she doesn't do Christmas, she celebrates spring. The rules of porch time, posted on a plaque, decree that festivities shall cease at 6:30, unless conversation is especially spirited, in which case an hour's extension is granted. The drinks are of fine stock and to order, the snacks copious.

Discussions vary as widely as the guests—affairs of state and nation, the weather, world travel and garbage collection, who runs the town and who pretends to, which neighbors are feuding, where to get your car or your teeth fixed, and other valuable intelligence.

Always on duty to greet guests were Smiling Sam and Butterscotch Candy, Mary's plump and gregarious golden retrievers, her house dogs. On her tree farm a few miles out of town were the farm dogs—Frisky, a matronly German shepherd who ran the place, her overgrown silvery son Shadow, and Honey, a doleful-eyed Chihuahua in a beagle body who was one of Mary's welfare cases, found badly injured and brought back to health and a happy home.

Mary is known around town as the "animal lady," an appellation she has not sought but perpetuates because she can't help herself. Morning may find a litter of kittens or a puppy abandoned on her doorstep, dropped by sneaks who salve weak consciences by unburdening their problem on "someone who will give them a good home." Any hour of day or night she may get a call from police or townspeople concerned about some wounded cat, starving horses, or dog chained in the hot sun without water. Madison's animal control officer is one who takes

There's just no way to avoid getting soaked when giving a German shepherd a bath. (Photograph © Jeff and Alexa Henry)

Though the German shepherd breed officially dates back about a century, a dog quite similar to the modern German shepherd existed as far back as the seventh century in what is today Germany. (Photograph © Isabelle Francais)

his job description literally and can't be found when an animal needs help, not control. So Mary keeps her car trunk provisioned with blankets, food, water, and first-aid equipment and she has developed a cadre of other caring persons to help out. Before long I was one.

I came to see Mary as the consummate dog person, golden retriever class. Before Sam and Scotch there had been Yo Yo, a prize winner and companion when Mary was an accountant with a big auditing firm in Washington and Indianapolis. Before Yo Yo there was Big Billy, who had won her heart to golden retrievers.

Mary's house is dogproofed—bric-a-brac kept on high shelves, carpets of color close to dog fur, inscribed feeding bowls, dog doors to the fenced-in yard, washable covers on couch and chairs, where snoozing is permitted except when company comes. One chair is a favorite for both Scotch and Sam. When Scotch has occupancy, Sam will slyly approach Mary for a little affection. Seeing scratching being administered, envious Scotch will get down to go for her share, whereupon Sam sneaks over to claim the chair, already well warmed.

Mary's canine family reminded me that a dogless life is a truncated life. Years of travel and no-pet apartments had separated me from the civilizing influence of dogs. My last benefactor had been Penny, a Dalmatian with a black eye acquired when I achieved the status of head of a family of three kids and a house in the suburbs. A dog was needed to complete the picture.

Penny was the only dog I ever bought, $20 as the runt of the litter. She grew to become what my son called "aristocratic," fiercely loyal and protective, with an uncanny capacity to relate differently and equally to each member of the family. She made daily rounds to steal from cat dishes and collect handouts from neighbors who missed her if she didn't come around. Penny was my companion on late-night walks, when I did my profound thinking. She'd go about her private prowlings and all but disappear until we reached a corner, where we met by agreement so I could see us safely across the street for another block of private prowling and profound thinking.

"Well," said Mary in a put-up-or-shut-up tone, "when do you want to go and see Amigo?"

She had picked out the dog for me, matched me and Amigo, a German shepherd at the vet's awaiting proper placement. I hesitated, by habit concerned that my work might involve travel, which Mary dispatched by offering to keep the dog while I was gone. My wariness over the apartment being too small and traffic too near were not worthy of response. Mary sensed that Amigo was a dog I couldn't resist.

She was right. At Dr. Petscher's, Amigo was a sudden black presence moving excitedly from one of us to the other, tail aswish. A magnificent creature! I wasn't prepared for a homeless dog of such beauty. All black except for brown-tan lower legs and white markings on shoulders and throat. Ears perked in the alertness of German shepherds. Moving in grace.

Facing page: *A curious shepherd pup gets a look at cattle for the first time. (Photograph © Jeff and Alexa Henry)*

She had been the sole companion of an elderly man who had died on Christmas Day. His relatives didn't want the dog, took her to the vet with instructions to put her to sleep—a full blood, only two years old. Dr. Petscher offered to find her a home.

Mary stood aside while I admired Amigo. No need to put the question: Do you want her? Who wouldn't?

I said I wanted to think it over, knowing all manner of thinking wouldn't change the outcome. For a week or so I did think it over, while shopping for dog dishes, leashes, chow and other canine paraphernalia.

It was a cold day in January when I went to collect her. She came along agreeably enough on the leash and got into the back seat of the car without fuss. But once I drove away she began scrambling from window to window, panting in fright. I talked, trying to calm her. She scurried back and forth, seeking escape. Her breath fogged over the windows and I had to wipe off the windshield to see.

Once home, her anxiety subsided only when she found refuge under the kitchen table. She hovered there, withdrawn against the wall, bewildered.

All my reticence about keeping her was gone. Amigo was not sure, but I was committed.

2

Amigo just laid there in the corner under the kitchen table for hours, day and night. Hunched down on her belly, head on her paws, ears laid back. She followed me with her eyes—furtive, suspicious. If I approached, she lifted her head as if bracing to defend herself.

"It's all right, girl," I'd say and stroke her lustrous black fur, scratch behind her ears. She tolerated this but when I quit she seemed relieved. She had been so friendly at the vet's, now she was leery of me.

I put food and water in bowls on the floor across the room but they went untouched. I moved the bowls over under the table beside her; she ignored them. She did lie on the rug I put down for her, as if it were part of her refuge. When in the house, she never moved from her tiny corner of security.

Only outside did she show any spirit. If I approached her with the leash, she responded; a walk must have meant a chance at freedom. She'd follow along sullenly, showing interest only in the scent markings on trees and bushes, a cat hiding under a car or barking by other dogs. Once back home, she fled to her place under the table.

After a few days her food showed nibble marks where she had tried it. I gave her milk, which she was too anxious to keep down.

She never barked, ever. Occasionally at night I would hear her flop down, changing positions. I never heard her scratch. Amigo was giving me the silent treatment.

We were in the bonding period, which the vet had said would take about 60 days. I was to keep her close; owner and pet need time to adjust to each other.

An organization in California that matches and trains dogs and people with disabilities has a seven-day "leash-up" period when human and animal are literally leashed together all day and all night—eating, sleeping, dressing, working, traveling, doing everything (yes, everything) within five feet of each other. It's make or break; the forced intimacy may reveal quickly that the two don't fit. If the bind-bond takes, the two are off to a wondrous partnership.

Amigo was no pliant puppy. She was two years old, fully grown and imprinted with past loyalties and learnings unknown to me. I was patient but yearned for her acceptance. As I worked alone upstairs at night, I was keen to the presence of a dog in the house and sometimes found myself saying her name, "Amigo . . . Amigo." A minor mistranslation of the Spanish—female "friend" would be Amiga—but a pleasing sound and I wanted its meaning to be true.

We took walks two, three or more times every day, in every weather. The bracing cold stimulated and cheered us. We ventured into 14-below numbness one still night, mutually agreed to abbreviate our outing and raced home to the warm relief of the house.

Occasionally at day's end after we had shared the brisk outdoors and I sat at my desk attempting to work I'd feel a sad separation from her, asleep downstairs under the kitchen table. Then I'd rouse her for another walk.

Soon we knew the turf and bark of every canine guardian along our way. Our approach set off the territorial alarm system when the duty dog challenged us, alerting another down the block who signaled the next, until the entire security force was on the lookout for approaching intruders.

I bought a longer leash to give Amigo greater range. By looping the end around one hand and playing it out as needed through the other, I managed both freedom and control. Training was not my purpose in these excursions, so I let her lead. I took charge of strategy (which direction to go, how far, and so on) and she decided tactics (where to stop for investigation and how long).

As the weather moderated and more people were about, Amigo drew the admiring comment, "Pretty dog," repeated with monotonous predictability. I was proud strolling with such a raven beauty.

Amigo doesn't have the classic conformation of the German shepherd—deep, muscular chest and long, low-slung hindquarters. She's almost svelte, with the slight-strong legs of a dancer, a sable silhouette flowing from pricked-up ears to her tall tapered tail, a creature of grace.

This pup has certainly found a good home. (Photograph © David F. Clobes, Stock Photography)

She has wiry strength, I learned when some bold cat would dart across our path and Amigo lunged, yanking the leash taut and pulling me after her. She took intense interest in Misty, the next-door cat, who was equally interested in Amigo. When Misty walked by outside, curious and teasing, Amigo dashed to the French doors, which give a dog's-eye view of the yard, and whimpered in frustration. I was glad for such vitality, a sign she was emerging from her malaise.

Amigo's reaction to kids was puzzling. She was wary when we approached them and cowered close to me when they surrounded us, accepting their pats uncomfortably. If we came upon a playground of boys shooting baskets, she crouched and pulled back in panic. Fear seized her whenever we came within earshot of a bouncing ball or the shrill shouts of children.

If a passing car backfired, I had to hold firmly to keep her from running wild. She was spooked, bad memories were working in her. Those frightening episodes may have driven her closer to me. I gave in to her need to flee from what menaced her, then drew her to a stop and talked to her, knelt down, tried to calm and reassure her. Back home, when she'd regained her security corner, she would look up at me, still shaken, as if grateful to be home with me. Once or twice when I told her good night as I left her to go to bed, she wagged her tail, ever so slightly.

Our outings must have been new adventures for Amigo. Her life before had been limited to staying home all day while her owner worked, then a walk in a nearby cemetery. We expanded our explorations to new parts of town.

Alleys became our preferred route; they were more intriguing and informative. People encountered in front, sitting on the porch or watering a well-kept lawn, were stiffer, their greetings grudging. Here, too, was the No-Pee Patrol: "Don't you let that dog do anything in my yard."

Life is not so restricted out back. Pretensions seem to fall away with the exposure of unkempt sheds and littered garages, trash, gardens gone to weeds, intimate apparel on clotheslines. Householders come upon in the act of cleaning up some mess are informal, open to talk. As conversation moves from weather or the task at hand I am regularly asked, "Are you from Madison?" I came to recognize this was not casual conversation but social reconnaissance, the small-town equivalent of "Halt! Who goes there?" The answer identifies one as friend or foe.

Partially to escape such scrutiny we took to open country for our daytime jaunts and walked the streets at night when residents had gone indoors. Late night was our favorite time, when vans and pickups were parked and people had gone to bed. A strange and wonderful silence settled on the streets. Nature came forth: cats on the prowl, dogs barking more in greeting than warning, a rabbit or possum scampering across an alley, crickets in concert and birds murmuring in the trees.

German shepherds may be one of the most intelligent breeds, but, like dogs everywhere, they get quite excited about chasing a tennis ball. (Photograph © Barbara von Hoffmann)

You could hear your footsteps crunching in leaves or snow.

One clear frigid night we sighted the dark figure of a woman emerging from an alley. She made for us, tottering, her coat carelessly open to the cold. The smell of booze preceded her and her greeting was slurred. Out of courtesy we stopped and soon were drawn into the loquacious soliloquy of the lonely drunk. She had a dog, too, but not much of one. She had a husband; he was not much either. She lived nearby, I couldn't make out where. She had questions but hardly heard my answers.

    Amigo tugged at the leash to get going. I began my parting comments and suddenly the woman moved forward and kissed me, soundly, right on the lips!

    I was stunned. A safe distance away, I reconnoitered. This must be a real friendly town.

Amigo welcomed her snug, warm corner after our foray in the cold. As I snuggled under the blankets I heard the sound of something moving in the dark. It was Amigo, walking around in my bedroom. I waited and listened. I heard her flop down in a corner near my bed. Until now she had never slept anywhere but under the kitchen table. I switched on the night-table lamp to check. She never moved, only opened her eyes for a moment and then closed them, settled for sleep.

    I turned off the light and lay in the dark, quietly thrilled.

The bond between people and their German shepherds is strong; who wouldn't want such a beautiful breed by their side? (Photograph © Kelly Vickery)

The Two Tulips

by J. R. Ackerley

Dogs can be baffling creatures, and German shepherds are no exception. They can easily create relative chaos from the most mundane circumstances. But as J. R. Ackerley illustrates in "The Two Tulips," Alsatians (as the British called German shepherds until the 1970s) can be well understood by looking at the world through their eyes.

J. R. Ackerley served as the editor of the British literary magazine the *Listener* for nearly a quarter century beginning in the mid-1930s. He is best known as an editor rather than a writer. However, he wrote several plays and books, including the drama *The Prisoners of War*, which is considered one of the best plays inspired by World War I, and *My Father Myself,* an autobiography that includes frank discussions about the author's homosexuality and his troubled family life.

"The Two Tulips" is taken from Ackerley's loving portrayal of his German shepherd, *My Dog Tulip* (1965).

A German shepherd takes a break on a bench. (Photograph © Roxanne Kjarum)

SOME YEARS AGO, when I was walking with my dog in Fulham Palace Gardens, we overtook an old woman who was wheeling a baby carriage. She was chatting cheerfully to the occupant of it, and it was therefore, perhaps, not unreasonable of me to be surprised to find, when I caught up with her, that this too was a dog. He was lying upon his back, propped up by pillows, with a rug tucked round his middle; just above the top of the rug the edge of a thick bandage was visible. Very comfortable and peaceful the little dog looked as the old woman trundled him along among the flowers, chatting to him in that bright, encouraging way in which people address invalids.

I made some sympathetic remark to her as I passed, and she was all agog to tell me about her troubles, how the poor little dog had been so seriously ill with an internal tumor, but how he was well on the road to recovery now, thanks, oh thanks—she could not thank her enough—to the wonderful lady vet who had operated on him and been so clever and so kind, for had it not been for her, the little dog, who was such a good little dog, would undoubtedly have died.

'Wouldn't you, love?' said she to the invalid, who lay back motionless against the pillows, with his paws folded on his stomach and a very solemn expression on his small pointed face.

This conversation made a deep impression upon me. I was then quite new to the dog world, for my present dog was the first I had ever possessed, and there was much that I did not know and wished to learn. It astounded me to hear that dogs underwent major operations and had their stomachs opened and shut as we do, and I tried to picture this little mongrel lying upon the operating table, under the glare of the head-lamps, with the grave faces of surgeons, nurses, and anaesthetists bent over him. What on earth would happen to my dog, I wondered uneasily, if she should ever develop anything so serious as an internal tumor? Who would care to operate on her? Before parting from the old woman, I did not fail to take the name and address of the lady vet who had been 'so clever and so kind.'

My own dog is an Alsatian bitch. Her name is Tulip. Alsatians have a bad reputation; they are said to bite the hand that feeds them. Indeed Tulip bit my hand once, but accidentally; she mistook it for a rotten apple we were both trying to grab simultaneously. One of her canines sank into my thumb-joint to the bone: when I held it under the tap afterwards I could see the sinews exposed. We all make mistakes and she was dreadfully sorry. She rolled over on the grass with all her legs in the air; and later on, when she saw the bandage on my hand, she put herself in the corner, the darkest corner of the bedroom, and stayed there for the rest of the afternoon. One can't do more than that.

But if you look like a wild beast you are expected to behave like one; and human beings, who tend to disregard the savagery of their own conduct, shake their heads over the Alsatian dog. 'What can you expect of a wolf?' they say.

Facing page: *A German shepherd keeps an eye on roof shovelers in Yellowstone National Park, a region with some dramatic snowfalls. (Photograph © Jeff and Alexa Henry)*

The German shepherd's trademark pointy ears with a broad base are readily apparent on this dog wading in a California pond. (Photograph © Sharon Eide/Elizabeth Flynn)

Tulip made no conspicuous effort to improve this situation. If people were inclined to look at her askance she gave them every reason to do so. They distrusted her; she suspected them. In fact she repudiated the human race altogether—that is to say the remainder of it. *I* could do with her whatever I wished—except stop her barking at other people. In this matter, she seemed to say, she knew better than I. Yet she behaved always with exemplary dignity and good breeding wherever she went, so long as she was let alone: it was when anyone approached her, or even gave the impression of being about to approach her, that she spoke her mind. She spoke sharply and loud, and she had a good deal to say, though what precisely her mind was I did not know. In truth, although I was very anxious to know, I was less anxious to find out. Her sweetness and gentleness to myself were such that it was almost impossible for me to believe that these were not the prevailing characteristics of her nature; but the language she used to others certainly sounded pretty strong, and bad language, as is well known, does not always stop at that.

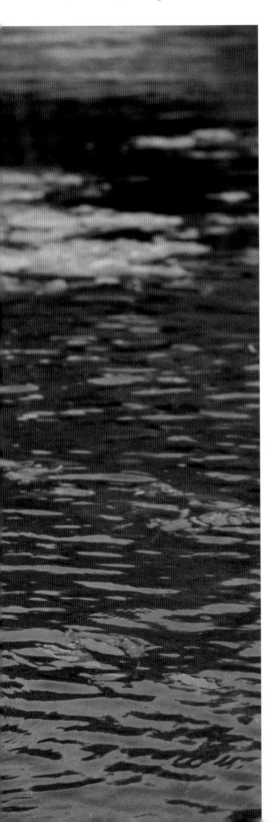

No doubt the reason why I took the constant care I did take to protect her from being put to the test of showing how far she would go, was that I had to admit I had an inkling; but the two bus conductors and the postman whom she had already bitten could hardly be accepted as a true sociological sample of her feelings for mankind. They had all been doing things, like coming soundlessly upon us in sneakers, or striking the bus a sudden sharp rat-tat alongside us with their ticket racks to make it move on, of which it is in the nature of dogs to disapprove; in any case she had not hurt them, but merely taken them by the sleeve or by the arm; and though one of the conductors had rolled back his cuff to display the wound, he himself seemed disappointed that there was nothing to be seen but a small white dent in his flesh.

When children are called difficult the cause is often traced to their homes, and it was upon Tulip's first home that I blamed her unsociable conduct. She had originally belonged to some working-class people who, though fond of her in their way, seldom took her out. She was too excitable, and too valuable, to be allowed off the leash; on it she pulled. For nearly a year she scarcely left their house, but spent her time, mostly alone, for they were at work all day, in a tiny backyard. She could hardly be expected, therefore, to learn the ways of a world she so rarely visited; the only 'training' she ever received was an occasional thrashing for the destruction which her owners discovered when they returned home. Alsatians in particular do not take kindly to beatings; they are too intelligent and too nervous. It was from this life, when she was eighteen months old, that I rescued her, and to it that I attributed the disturbances of her psyche. Thereafter it was clear that if she could have her way she would never let me out of her sight again.

It is necessary to add that she is beautiful. People are always wanting to touch her, a thing she cannot bear. Her ears are tall and pointed, like the ears of Anubis. How she manages to hold them constantly erect, as though starched, I do not know, for with their fine covering of mouse-gray fur they are soft and flimsy; when she stands with her back to the sun it shines through the delicate tissue, so that they glow shell-pink as though incandescent. Her face also is long and pointed, basically stone-gray but the snout and lower jaw are jet black. Jet, too, are the rims of her amber eyes, as though heavily mascara'd, and the tiny mobile eyebrow tufts that are set like accents above them. And in the midst of her forehead is a kind of Indian caste-mark, a black diamond suspended there, like the jewel on the brow of Pegasus in Mantegna's 'Parnassus,' by a fine dark thread, no more than a pencilled line, which is drawn from it right over her poll midway between the tall ears. A shadow extends across her forehead from either side of this caste-mark, so that, in certain lights, the diamond looks like the body of a bird with its wings spread, a bird in flight.

These dark markings symmetrically divide up her face into zones of pale pastel colors, like a mosaic, or a stained-glass window; her skull, bisected by the thread, is two primrose pools, the center of her face light gray, the bridge of her nose above the long, black lips fawn, her cheeks white, and upon each a *patte de mouche* has been tastefully set. A delicate white ruff, frilling out from the lobes of her ears, frames this strange, clownish face, with its heavily leaded features, and covers the whole of her throat and chest with a snowy shirt front.

For the rest, her official description is sable-gray: she is a gray dog wearing a sable tunic. Her gray is the gray of birch bark; her sable tunic is of the texture of satin and clasps her long body like a saddle-cloth. No tailor could have shaped it more elegantly; it is cut round the joints

German shepherd siblings get a ride. (Photograph © Marilyn "Angel" Wynn)

A puppy in a basket. (Photograph © Sharon Eide/Elizabeth Flynn)

of her shoulders and thighs and in a straight line along the points of her ribs, lying open at the chest and stomach. Over her rump it fits like a cap, and then extends on in a thin strip over the top of her long tail down to the tip. Viewed from above, therefore, she is a black dog; but when she rolls over on her back she is a gray one. Two dark ribbons of fur, descending from her tunic over her shoulders, fasten it at her sternum, which seems to clip the ribbons together as with an ivory brooch.

She had been to three vets already for various reasons. It was a measure of my naïveté in dog affairs that my first consultation with a vet was to inquire whether she was in heat. The question was never settled, that is to say by him, for when he was finally able to make himself heard, in his bleak surgery, above her deafening challenge and my own vain exhortations to her to calm herself, all he said, in a cold voice, was, 'Have you any control over your dog?'

In the face of the evidence it seemed idle to return anything but 'No'; to which, still keeping his distance, he drily replied, 'Then take her out of my surgery at once.'

Some weeks later she sustained a small cut in one of her pads, which took so long to heal that I began to fear that it would never heal at all; another vet had been recommended to me, and I decided to try my luck with him. He was an ex-Army man, a Major, and the most that I asked of Tulip on this occasion was that she should allow me to flex her paw so that, without touching her, he could glance at the cut. But she would not permit even that. Having failed, as I had failed, to humor her or shout her down, the Major suddenly lost his temper, and exclaiming, 'These

Alsatians! They're all the same!' he swooped upon her and beat her about the body with his bare hands.

These dashing military tactics were not without effect; they drove her, trembling with astonishment and fear, beneath his operating table, from the shelter of which she looked out at him with an expression which I might secretly excuse but could not approve; but they did not enable him to examine her, if that was part of his plan, and they could hardly be construed as an invitation to call again. They implied also, I took it, a rebuke to myself, as well as the more obvious one they meted out to her; they were teaching me a much needed lesson in how to discipline an unruly dog: 'Spare the rod and spoil the child!' was what the Major was, in effect, saying.

As I walked away from this establishment with Tulip, who was now in her gayest and most winning mood, I supposed myself to be in possession of an undoctorable dog; but this gloomy reflection was succeeded by two others of a more comforting nature. The first was that, after all, she hadn't bitten the Major. And he might truly be said to have asked for that. Flinging caution to the winds, he had set about her; but she had not retaliated: whatever savagery had been exhibited in the surgery had not been exhibited by her. My other reflection was, in one way, even more comforting. 'These Alsatians! They're all the same!' he had said. Tulip, then, was not exceptional in her tiresomeness. She was not, so to speak, a delinquent dog. If all Alsatians were the same, her peculiarities were of the breed and not an individual affair. But if all Alsatians were the same, did any of them ever receive medical attention?

It transpired that they did; and above all the conflicting emotions that rent me when we visited our third vet—this time for a most important service, to have her inoculated against distemper—was gratitude that he did not summon the police or the fire department. I had made the appointment by telephone, and had thought it politic to apologise for Tulip in advance and to explain that, although I did not believe there was really any harm in her, she was not the most amenable of patients. To this the vet had merely grunted: when I set out with her I was already unnerved by the thought of the struggle that lay ahead. Nor were my drooping spirits raised by the first sight that greeted us, a Spaniel who was being treated as we arrived. This creature was visible to us, like some callous admonishment, before ever we reached the surgery door, for its window looked out upon a yard through which we had to pass, and the Spaniel was all too plainly seen within.

He was standing quietly on a table with a thermometer sticking out of his bottom, like a cigarette. And this humiliating spectacle was rendered all the more crushing by the fact that there was no one else there. Absolutely motionless, and with an air of deep absorption, the dog was standing upon the table in an empty room with a thermometer in his bottom, almost as though he had put it there himself.

'Oh, Tulip!' I groaned. 'If only you were like that!'

But she was not. When the vet returned from his dispensary and,

Facing page: A typical German shepherd: poised, self-confident, fearless—and a little playful. (Photograph © Isabelle Francais)

THE WA
Smoke Alarm
Crash of Swissair 111
Stirs Debate on When
To Stick to Procedure
Some Argue for Improvising
During an Emergency
To Cut Down on Delays
What's News
World-Wide

An elderly shepherd holds the Wall Street Journal *for its owner. (Photograph © Marilyn "Angel" Wynn)*

the thermometer and the spaniel having been successively removed, was free to turn his attention to us, she was not in the least like that. Suspecting the place's character, no doubt, from the pervasive odor of medicaments and the howls and moans of the various sick animals penned in the kennel at the back, she had exhibited the strongest aversion to entering it, and was now imploring and cajoling me to take her away: as soon as the vet opened his mouth to speak, she replied. A gray little man with an unsmiling face, he stood with his syringe in his hand patiently waiting while I petted and coaxed poor Tulip, speaking soothingly to her in baby language, as she shrank, dribbled, and barked between my knees.

'Can you turn her back to me and hold her head still?' he inquired, in a momentary lull.

'I think so,' I said nervously.

But to turn her back on this odious little man was the last thing that Tulip intended; she squirmed convulsively out of my grasp over and over again, eventually wrenching her head out of her collar. Under the vet's expressionless gaze I had to retrieve her and rebuckle it, with hands which, he probably noticed, shook as much as she did.

'May I give her the injection myself?' I asked. 'You could show me where to do it and she wouldn't mind it from me.'

The vet made no reply. Instead, he laid his syringe upon the table, rang the bell, selected a strip of bandage from a hook on the wall and made a loop in it—all without a word. The door opened, and an assistant came in.

'Good!' exclaimed the vet to me, with sudden briskness. 'Now just keep her head like that for a moment!' and advancing the loop towards Tulip, who was still determinedly pointing her face at him, and now glared at the approaching contraption as though mesmerised, he abruptly noosed her nose, with what was plainly the dexterity of long practice, drew her jaws tightly and roughly together, turned the ends of the tape round her throat and knotted them behind her ears.

'Oh, I say!' I cried. 'Don't hurt her! There's really no need.'

I was, indeed, in no position, or even mind, to question whatever methods this busy and helpful man might think fit to employ to exercise over my animal the control I lacked, and my miserable ejaculation was only wrung from me by the sight of Tulip's horror-stricken face and the squawk of pain and despair she uttered before her powers of speech were cut rudely short.

My thoughts, in fact, were in the utmost confusion. I suffered to see my dear, affectionate dog ill-used, but I could hardly expect my tender feelings to be shared by a vet who was meeting her for the first time and clearly did not bring out in her, like myself, the sweetest and the best. What should I do, I pondered, if I were in his shoes, confronted with a strange, large, vulpine, and unfriendly dog, possessed of an excellent set of teeth, into whom I was asked to stick a needle? Would I cheerfully grasp her with hands upon the wholeness of which my

Facing page: *The breed's calm demeanor and loving personality have made the German shepherd a favorite for therapy visits to hospitals and retirement homes. Here a white German shepherd gets a much-appreciated scratch between the ears from an elderly woman. (Photograph © Marilyn "Angel" Wynn)*

means of livelihood depended? Yet, on the other side, could it be good for a creature, already so nervous and mistrustful, to be subjected to such violent stratagems?

However, for all the attention the vet paid me, I might never have spoken. 'Now, Bob!' was all he said, and, brushing me aside, he and his assistant took hold of the defenceless Tulip, who was foaming at the mouth with terror, and pulling her legs from beneath her, brought her heavily to the ground.

'Pass the syringe,' said the vet.

After this, my ambition in life was to keep Tulip in such a state of health that she need never visit a vet again. It was an ambition which she herself appeared to share. She would not, if she could help it, even enter the streets in which her last two experiences had taken place. If I happened to forget and turned down one of them when we were out, I would suddenly miss her from my side, an unheard-of thing, and looking wildly round, espy her far behind me, motionless at the corner, staring after me with her exclamation-mark face. There is no getting away from Tulip's face; with its tall ears constantly focused upon one it demands an attention which it seems unremittingly to give. She fixes one, as one is sometimes claimed and fixed by those insistent bores who, when they have something to impart, hold one's gaze with a searching, inescapable stare, as though they know from experience that the attention of their listeners is apt to wander and are determined to exact that responsive gleam of intelligence which their remorseless personalities require. 'Are you listening?' they say, irritably or plaintively, from time to time.

Tulip's face perpetually said the same thing, for with all its perpendicular lines, the tall ears, the long nose, the black streak down the forehead and the little vertical eyebrow tufts, it was not merely interrogatory but exclamatory also: it said both 'What?' and 'What!' Useless to call her now, she would not budge; I must return to her and reach my objective by another route; but later I discovered that she would consent to follow me down these unsavory roads so long as I reassured her, by passing the surgeries, that it was not my intention to enter them. Then she would come, but always with infinite distaste, crossing the road to make the widest possible detour and hurrying past the baleful buildings, casting at them every now and then a repugnant, sidelong glance.

But my disinclination to visit vets was in frequent conflict with my need to consult them; perplexities of all sorts troubled my ignorant and anxious mind, and not the least of my worries at the time of my encounter with the old woman in Fulham Palace Gardens was that, in spite of the nourishing food I provided, Tulip looked too thin; beneath her sable tunic all her ribs were visible. The distressing word 'Worms' was dropped into my ear by a kind acquaintance, and soon afterwards I

decided to take her along to see Miss Canvey, which was the name of
the lady vet who bad been 'so clever and so kind.' Her surgery was in
Parsons Green, and to the kennel maid who answered the phone I
explained, in the apologetic manner which was now habitual with me,
that my bitch was very difficult and I would prefer, if convenient, to
bring her along out of surgery hours.

Miss Canvey was a short, thickset, young woman with bobbed hair,
spectacles, and a homely peasant's face. She wore a white overall, not
intimidatingly clean, and as she advanced across the large, bare room
towards me, I took an impression of calmness and competence. I had
spoken sternly to Tulip as we waited, exhorting her to good behavior
for a change, but I had no expectation of any improvement and there
was none; she accorded Miss Canvey her usual defiant reception—
defiance which became the more emphatic the more it was ignored.
Miss Canvey approached imperturbably and stood quietly in front of us,
looking down at her, while I stumbled through some account of her
past and present troubles, punctuated with irritable commands to the
dog to pipe down.

'She's like this with everyone,' I said ruefully, 'but as sweet as pie to
me. I can't make it out.'

Miss Canvey did not speak, but continued to gaze down at the
excited animal. Then she asked:

'What's her name?' I told her. 'Well Tulip, you *are* a noisy girl, aren't
you? What's it all about?' and she extended her hand, back foremost.
Tulip paused for a moment to sniff it, then, as the hand was moved
closer, retreated, barking more violently than ever. How maddening,
how intolerable it was that this creature, usually so attentive and obedient to my wishes, should always let me down in public in this stupid
way! Suddenly yelling 'Stop it, you brute!' I biffed her on the nose. The
blow was harder than I intended. Tulip gave a little cry of pain and
rubbed her nose with her paw. Then she rose up on her hind legs and
gently licked my face.

'I see,' said Miss Canvey promptly. 'You're the trouble.'

'I?' I exclaimed, astonished.

'Just slip the lead through her collar, will you. I'll examine her in
another room.'

'Are you sure it will be all right?' I asked anxiously, doing as I was
bid.

'Perfectly all right.' And twisting the lead round her strong wrist,
she marched firmly out of the room, towing behind her the horrified
and struggling Tulip who cast back at me agonized glances as she slid
and sprawled across the linoleum. The door closed.

Alone in the surgery I listened apprehensively for sounds—screams
from Miss Canvey, cries of pain or rage from Tulip, rushing feet, banging doors—sounds of any sort: none could be reassuring. But the place
was as silent as the grave. Then, after what seemed an eternity but was

only ten minutes, I heard a scuffling in the passage and a few barks, but of a very different timbre; the door opened and Tulip reappeared, this time with Miss Canvey in tow.

'No sign of worms,' remarked the latter, dropping the lead. 'She's in excellent condition.'

'How did she behave?' I asked, while Tulip cast herself into my arms and lavished upon me a greeting more suitable in its extravagance to lovers who had been parted for years.

'Good as gold,' said Miss Canvey.

'Did you tie up her nose?'

'Heavens, no! I never do that.'

'But you had help?' I said, gazing mistily at her.

Miss Canvey smiled:

'Of course not. She was no trouble. I knew she wouldn't be.'

'How did you know?' I asked humbly.

'Well, you learn by experience, I suppose. But it isn't difficult to tell a dog's character from its face. Tulip's a good girl, I saw that at once. You're the trouble.'

I sat down.

'Do tell me,' I said.

'Well, she's in love with you, that's obvious. And so life's full of worries for her. She has to protect you to begin with; that's why she's upset when people approach you: I expect she's a bit jealous, too. But in order to protect you she's naturally got to be free; that's why she doesn't like other people touching her; she's afraid, you see, that they may take hold of her and deprive her of her freedom to guard you. That's all the fuss is about, I should say. It's you she's thinking of. But when you're not there, there's nothing for her to do, of course, and no anxiety. Anyone can handle her then. I'm sure. That's all,' she concluded with a smile. 'Dog's aren't difficult to understand. One has to put oneself in their position.'

Miss Canvey could have put herself in any position she wished, for I was already her slave and gazed at her with the veneration with which we behold a saint. I asked her some questions about Tulip's diet, paid the fee—half-a-crown, so far as I recall, was all that this miracle cost—and took my leave. As I was going, she suddenly said:

'Why do you shout at her?'

'I don't know,' I stammered, rather taken aback. 'She exasperates me sometimes. She doesn't seem to hear what I say.'

'She can hear a pin drop!' said Miss Canvey briefly. 'Look at her ears!' Then on a milder note: 'Try not to. It's bad for her. She's very highly strung. Speak to her quietly; she'll do anything you want in time.'

As we walked away I apologised to Tulip for hitting her on her beautiful nose, and, in my thoughts, for much else besides. In the light of Miss Canvey's interpretation, how infinitely more hideous that abject struggle in the last vet's surgery now seemed, how heroic her conduct,

Facing page: *German shepherds shed profusely; even owners quite diligent with the brush will find furballs lurking in every corner of their lives. (Photograph © Marilyn "Angel" Wynn)*

how mean and contemptible mine. I had apologised for her devotion, and then betrayed it. I recollected, with a shudder, how I had held her head still for the approaching trap. I felt very tender towards her.

After this, we may be said almost to have lived in the surgery of dear Miss Canvey, that Florence Nightingale of the animal world. I walked Tulip over to see her on any pretext, however trifling, and such was the confidence she inspired that very soon I no longer bothered to make special appointments, but dropped in during surgery hours and sat with Tulip in the crowded room awaiting our turn and watching wonderful Miss Canvey at work upon a miscellaneous assortment of sick dogs, cats, rabbits, and poultry. It was an enthralling and uplifting spectacle, and though her white overalls became less and less white and her bobbed hair more and more disordered, she never lost that air of calm authority which it was a positive tonic to breathe. That Tulip ever enjoyed these visits as much as I did, I cannot pretend; but my own freedom from anxiety no doubt affected her too; what resistance she put up seemed more perfunctory, and once inside, she sat by my knee quietly, except for an occasional mew of impatience, until her turn came. Then, of course, when the solid little figure of Miss Canvey approached us, she put on her act, though with less of the old conviction; with a genial word of welcome, Miss Canvey simply took the lead and towed her from the room.

One day I observed among the other pilgrims to this shrine a young working man with his Collie dog, which was muzzled. Miss Canvey was busily engaged in extracting a tintack from the anus of a hen, and it was some time before she noticed him. Then she called across the room:

'Why is your dog muzzled?'

'I don't trust 'im, Miss,' said the young man, blushing.

'Take it off,' said Miss Canvey.

She always spoke quietly, though sometimes, as now, rather abruptly; no one ever thought of disobeying her, and the young man complied. When his turn came she examined his dog with her usual coolness and thoroughness; then she took the young man aside and spoke earnestly to him in a corner. I could not catch what she said, but at the end of it he smiled and murmured 'Thank you, Miss.' Then he went off with his dog, carrying the muzzle in his hand.

While this little scene was being enacted, I happened to be sitting near the desk where Miss Canvey's kennel-maid was writing out prescriptions, and leaning over, I whispered to her:

'Has Miss Canvey ever been bitten?'

The kennel-maid looked cautiously round before replying; then she said, in a low, hesitant voice:

'Well, she has once, to my knowledge; but I don't think she'd like it known.'

'Please tell me.'

Four-year-old Celeste gets a face full of snow and immediately takes action to rectify the situation. (Photograph © Phil Marques)

'I didn't actually see it happen,' said the girl, 'because I was busy with something else; but I heard a sort of scuffle—it was another Collie she was treating, too—and saw her go quickly out of the room holding her hand. When she returned she had a bandage on her wrist, but she went back to finish what she'd been doing. I asked, "Did he bite you?" but all she said, rather shortly, was "It was my fault. I was clumsy." And though I offered to take over the case from her, and so did Mr. Mather when he got to hear of it, she would never let anyone else handle the dog all the time he was ill. He never hurt her again, and they became very good friends in the end.'

'Sublime woman!' I said.

The kennel-maid smiled:

'She's fond of animals, and so they like and trust her. All animals, but specially horses. They're what she likes best.'

Alas, it was true. She loved horses more than dogs, and so I have to speak of her in the past tense, for after we had enjoyed less than a year of her ministrations, her true love galloped her away into a country practice. Happy the horses wherever she is! But my own spirits went into the deepest mourning. Miss Canvey herself, I think, experienced a certain sense of guilt at abandoning us. Looking into my downcast face for the last time, she said:

'I'm not exceptional, you know.'

'You are to me,' I said, with a sigh.

Flushing a little, she said firmly:

'You can tell any vet from me that Tulip is perfectly all right. But she must always be examined away from you. It's you who cause the trouble. Tell them that. She's a nervous bitch, and you make her more nervous. But when you're out of the way anyone can handle her. You can tell them all that from me.'

Then she uttered the last words I was ever to hear from her lips, and which, although I was too stunned by the sickening blow they dealt me to take in their full implication at the time, afforded me, in retrospect, a glimpse, the most revealing I ever had, into the depths of her heart. Fixing me with a significant look, she said:

'Never let anyone feed Tulip but yourself!'

Dear Miss Canvey, she was a romantic, of course; yet with her rather matter-of-fact air of sturdy capability she managed to convey a quite different impression, and it was only after she had gone that I was able to perceive how profoundly romantic she was. Indeed, if she had stayed, I might never have perceived it at all, for how should I have known that the two different dogs she insisted upon my possessing, the Tulip who lived always at my side, and that other Tulip with whom she had made herself privately familiar, were, to all intents and purposes, the same? This concept of hers, in fact, that I was guarded by an unap-proachable tigress who became, in my absence, the meekest of lambs, had almost everything to recommend it; it worked and it pleased; it enchanted me, and so far as Miss Canvey herself was concerned, it appealed, I feel sure, to something so deep in her nature that I believe she might have gone to almost any lengths to keep the two Tulips apart. Moreover, a bewitching air of mystery enwrapped it; a transformation rite had to be performed, with Miss Canvey as High Priestess, and an act of faith was required on both sides; for just as I could never know Miss Canvey's Tulip except by repute, since she existed only in my absence, so it was an essential part of Miss Canvey's programme that she also must take—or rather leave—my Tulip for granted.

This may sound fanciful; but how else can her last terrible injunction be explained unless on the grounds that she wished to perpetuate the romantic situation which she herself had created and cherished, and which, she divined, satisfied in me, too, some profound psychological need? How truly those last insidious words found their mark! For I could not feed Tulip myself! I was too busy, and such offices, as Miss Canvey herself knew, were already in process of being delegated to a housekeeper, lately engaged for the purpose. Had I made a ghastly mistake? Was I now about to lose my Tulip, that savage lover and protector whom Miss Canvey had striven so hard to preserve for me intact? Should I find myself soon with Miss Canvey's Tulip, that reduced, spiritless, abject creature, anybody's stroke, while my housekeeper enjoyed the fierce flattery of mine? That this obsessive fear haunted my life for many months was proof enough how well Miss Canvey had sized me up. But—she would be the first to rejoice—she had not sized up Tulip. Indeed, how should human beings suspect in the lower beasts those noblest virtues which they themselves attain only in the realms of fiction? Tulip was incorruptible. She was constant. It mattered not who fed, flattered, or befriended her, or for how long; her allegiance never wavered; she had given her heart to me in the beginning, and mine, and mine only, it was to remain forever.

Miss Canvey therefore underrated her, and it was left to Mr. Brasenose of Brighton to whom I next had recourse for veterinary aid—Tulip's nails needed cutting—to imply that she had overrated her too. Mr. Brasenose was a cheerful young man who whistled while he worked, who continued to whistle, indeed, throughout Tulip's customary hostilities, and when I had recited to him Miss Canvey's magic formula, which I had learnt by heart, all he said was:

'Oh, I shouldn't bother to go. I expect Tulip would prefer you to stay.'

This was so far from being an aspect of the matter that had occurred to me, that it needed a moment or two to take it in; by the time I had focused it and, as it seemed to me, its total and reckless wrongheadedness, he had got his clippers out and was saying, 'Just hoist her on the table, will you?' in so casual a manner, as though she were a sack, that I found myself complying. The operation was not performed without difficulty; Mrs. Brasenose, indeed, had to be summoned by her husband from an inner apartment to help me prop Tulip up on the table and retrieve those various portions of her anatomy which, like the fringes of a jelly on too small a plate, kept escaping over the edge; but at any rate it was performed, by the merrily trilling vet, and with as little concern for Tulip's protests and struggles as if he had been cutting the nails of a mouse.

Thus opened another chapter of Tulip's medical history, and the last; although I continued faithfully to repeat my formula to all the vets we subsequently visited, none of them paid to it the least attention. This strange heedlessness upset me at first; not on their account, of course; if they chose to ignore Miss Canvey's advice, that was their lookout; but was it fair to Tulip to impose on her this additional strain of worrying about me when she had trouble enough of her own? Upon reflection, however, I was less sure; since the ruling passion of her life was to keep me always in her eye, might she not actually prefer me to stay?

Moreover, this new chapter, I gradually perceived, had one considerable advantage; it shed light upon the problem that had embarrassed my public life with Tulip from the start and which Miss Canvey had deliberately left unexplored: What was my Tulip really like? How far, in my presence, would she go? It turned out that she was Miss Canvey's Tulip—that is to say 'as good as gold.' This was what I had always believed, and what Miss Canvey herself had seemed to confirm when she said that she saw at a glance that Tulip was a 'good girl'—leaving, however, unclear in my mind to what lengths, in Miss Canvey's philosophy, a good girl might be permitted to go in defence of her man, or her horse.

Tulip was a good girl; but as I went on hoisting her up on to one surgery table after another and supporting her there while the vets took swabs of her womb, or, opening her scissor-like jaws with their bare hands, rammed yards of stomach-pump tubing down her throat, I experienced, besides gratitude and admiration for her self-restraint, a kind of nostalgia for the past. Life was becoming dull and prosaic; something had gone out of it with dear Miss Canvey, some enrichment, some fine flavor. And this, I then knew, was the very knowledge from which, in her wisdom, she had sought to protect me: the death of the legend, the disillusionment of the heart. My Tulip: had it not now to be admitted that she had been seen through, that her bluff had been called, her stature reduced? No tigress she, but—must I face it?—an ordinary dog. Was it not even possible that, in the course of time, under these civilizing processes, she would become so tame, so characterless, so commonplace, that she might one day be found standing in a surgery alone with a thermometer in her bottom?

Tulip never let me down. She is nothing if not consistent. She knows where to draw the line, and it is always in the same place, a

Some consider the German shepherd a breed to be feared, but this shepherd's gentle eyes reflect a kind soul. (Photograph © Marilyn "Angel" Wynn)

circle around us both. Indeed, she is a good girl, but—and this is the point—she would not care for it to be generally known. So wherever Miss Canvey may be—jogging, I hope, down some leafy lane upon a steed who will let no one mount him but herself—I would like her to know that Tulip is still the kind of good girl of whom she would approve. When, therefore, the little local boys ask me, as they often do, in their respectful and admiring way, though mistaking Tulip's gender: 'Does he bite, Mister?' I always return the answer which she, and Miss Canvey, would wish me to give.

The Dog with a Hollow Leg

by Ken W. Purdy

 German shepherds have often found employment with the military—in fact, the German army first used shepherds on the front lines during World War I, which brought the breed to the attention of the British and the Americans. As with soldiers in war, close contact between an infantryman and a dog during the horrors of battle creates a lasting bond, a special kind of love only the shepherd and the soldier truly understand.

Ken W. Purdy edited several national magazines including *Victory*, *Parade*, and *True*, and served as a contributing editor to *Playboy*, writing primarily about automobiles, from 1958 until his death in 1969. He also wrote more than a half dozen books about cars.

Here, Purdy writes of the special kind of soldier/German shepherd love created by war in his story "The Dog with a Hollow Leg," which first appeared in the *Saturday Evening Post* in 1961.

৵

German shepherds have a noble quality that is difficult to define in words; it is, however, unmistakable when you see it. (Photograph © Jeff and Alexa Henry)

"Man gets up around his sixties," my Uncle Martin said to me, "he ought to cultivate moderation. Shouldn't lose his temper so often. Eat less. Drink less. Particularly drink less. No man getting along for seventy can drink as much as he used to. No man. No dog, either, comes to that."

He held his glass of bourbon to the firelight and squinted through it. I didn't say anything. I wanted to think for a minute before I spoke, lest I be trapped into some outrageous display of ignorance or stupidity or both. I could recognize one of Uncle Martin's gambits when I heard it. He was a tricky old man. I wouldn't say he was a habitual liar, but I suspected that he came pretty close to the edge sometimes.

"I didn't know it was a problem for most dogs," I said cautiously.

"Lots you don't know, boy," Uncle Martin said. "Just for example, what would you think if you went into a man's house on a day he expected company and saw him take a half-full bottle of whisky to the kitchen sink and run water into it right up to the top? You'd think he was a pretty low fellow, wouldn't you? Well, wouldn't you?"

I admitted it.

"You'd be wrong!" Uncle Martin said. "Dead wrong! Fact of the matter is, in the case I'm thinking of, the man was doing a kindly, considerate thing, the act of a gentleman."

"Most people wouldn't think so," I said.

"The snap judgment is the bane of civilization," Uncle Martin said. "Let me tell you about this fella who was watering the whisky."

"Go ahead," I said. "I'd be glad to hear about it."

"Also you can't get *out* of hearing about it," Uncle Martin said. "Sit down and stop wiggling around."

"This is a young fella I'm thinking about," Uncle Martin said. "He might be thirty-five, thirty-six, name of Jerry Brainerd. You don't know him, and how I know him doesn't matter. I went around to see him one night—he had some other people coming too—and when I walked in the back way, there he was like I told you, running water into this whisky.

"Well, I said, 'Beg your pardon,' and tried to look away and back out and pretend I hadn't seen what he was doing, like you would if you saw a man jimmying open a poor box or something. But he was brazen as could be.

"'Hello, Martin,' he says. 'Come on in and have a chair. I'm just fixing up a couple bottles of whisky.'

'I can see you are,' I said. I suppose I must have sounded a little on the prim side, though I wasn't trying to. But that's a terrible thing to see. Terrible.

"Jerry laughed. 'I wasn't fixing it up for you,' he said. He lowered his voice and looked around like a burglar about to try a back window. 'It's for Mike,' he said.

"That's Jerry's dog, Mike. I'd seen him around, the once or twice I'd been to the house before. Big dog. German shepherd. I mean really big. I'd seen healthy heifers weren't as big as that dog.

The classic pose of a German shepherd against a golden backdrop. (Photograph © Barbara von Hoffmann)

"'I see,' I said. Of course I didn't at all.

"'I have to do it when he's not around,' Jerry said.

"'Naturally,' I said. 'Wouldn't do to let him catch you at it.' Meantime I was wondering if I ought to try to find out the name of his family doctor or something. But then I remembered my lifelong guiding principle, that things are practically never what they seem to be. So I sat down at the kitchen table, and when he got through with his nefarious deed, Jerry poured a couple of modest drinks out of an honest bottle and sat down with me.

"'I never told you about old Mike, did I?' Jerry says. 'I met old Mike in Korea in 1951, during that difference of opinion we had with the Chinese and others. I was a pressman's helper when I went into the Army, so they put me in the K-9 Corps and made a dog handler out of me. It seemed logical to somebody, and anyway the Army wasn't doing a lot of printing, I suppose. Actually I didn't mind. I like dogs. I suppose you know how it worked. Each handler worked a certain number of dogs, and in my bunch there was this monster shepherd, Michaelis von Eberhorst und Steblen. Naturally we called him Mike. He was the best dog in the outfit. He really was some dog. Anything you were smart enough to figure out a way to get into his head, he could learn. I know for a fact Mike killed three men, but he had a disposition like an angel. You wouldn't believe it to see him try to rip a set of leathers off a trainer and then trot back to me wagging his tail, and a big grin on his face.

"'When we went out on night patrol, the dog was point. That was the way we did it. Without the dog, in some of the country out there, a patrol could walk through a company of North Koreans or Chinese and never see one. The dog took care of that.

"'Mike was smart, as I've told you, and he was lucky. He saw a lot of action and he never got hurt. Patrols that went out with him were lucky too; at least I thought so, and of course I was always along, since I was Mike's handler.

"'One night, up around Kumsong, we went out about nine-thirty, an hour or so after dark. It was early in the fall, September, and it was a nice enough night, for Korea. We'd been out about an hour when old Mike hit the deck. Mike had his own way of working. The second he got a scent he'd drop like a rock and try to work out where it was coming from. That usually didn't take him long, but this one night he stayed down so long I began to wonder about him. We were in a tight little place, a hill on one side of us and a marshy little pond on the other. Finally I reached over and rubbed Mike behind the ears a little, and he decided to move. We hadn't made twenty feet when one of the guys let off a carbine, I heard a short scream and a grenade went off— in my pocket, it seemed to me, it was that close.

"'What had happened, there was a Chinese squatting in the water up to his neck, waiting for us, or somebody, or anybody. He was in the water to fool dogs, of course, but at that Mike had smelled a little corner of him. Lord knows how long that guy had been there, waiting for a chance to heave his grenades. But somebody had seen his arm come up, and the first one he threw was the last.

"'One had been enough: We had one man dead, another with a hole in his chest, and Mike was down—all ripped up, and he couldn't use his hind legs. I stuck a couple of bandages on him, which did no good at all, and then I picked him up, before the lieutenant could get any idea about leaving him behind. We brought them all in: the fellow who was killed, the guy hit in the chest and Mike.

"'The vets said Mike was hopeless. They wanted to shoot him. His back right leg was in terrible shape, two bones broken; he'd lost a tremendous amount of blood through my amateur bandages, but he was conscious, and he was as calm as a cigar-store Indian, not even whining.

"'I told the vets I wanted him fixed up, but they said nothing doing, they had nothing to use for anesthetic, and the shock of operating on him without it would kill him, they were sure of it. I'd have to let them shoot him, they told me.

The German shepherd search-and-rescue dog Hoss poses with a Yellowstone National Park ranger. German shepherds have dominated the canine field of search-and-rescue almost from its inception, due to their keen sense of smell and their overwhelming desire to please their owners and work hard. (Photograph © Jeff and Alexa Henry)

"'I made them give me half an hour, and I took off. I didn't waste any time trying to promote any morphine or ether or anything from the medics. I knew how it was with them. I just hoped they had enough for the guy we'd brought back. But I knew a chopper pilot who could promote a little whisky once in a while. I found him. He had two bottles of bonded bourbon. You know how much bonded bourbon was worth up there? Just a hundred and ten dollars a fifth. I told him it was an emergency and made a deal with him: both bottles for an even two hundred dollars.

"'I whipped back to the kennels. Mike was still alive and still conscious. I told the two vets the proposition: one bottle for the dog, one for them. They looked at each other, and one of them told the other to get some penicillin. While they were setting up to operate, I had a little talk with Mike. I couldn't figure

A shepherd plays in the Pacific surf near Monterey, California. (Photograph © Frank S. Balthis)

out any way to get it across to him what we were trying to do, but he knew well enough that I wanted to help him, and when I started pouring that bottle of whisky down his throat, at least he didn't take my arm off at the elbow, which he could have down just by closing his mouth.

"'It took those two clowns, working fast, an hour and a half to stitch Mike together. Whenever he showed any sign that he felt anything I'd pour another ounce of whisky into him. In the course of the operation, believe it or not, I gave him the whole bottle except for about an inch in the bottom— that and a couple of shots I took myself.

It won't be long before this owner will no longer be able to lift her rapidly enlarging German shepherd pup. (Photograph © Jeff and Alexa Henry)

"'I saved what was left, and it was a good thing I did, because when I went around to see Mike in the morning, he was sick as a dog, so to speak; he had what I'm willing to bet was the worst hang-over any dog ever had since time began. I gave him a little hair of the man that bit him, and he seemed to rally. I know he appreciated it.

"'Mike never worked again, of course, but he got well. He had what you might call an uneventful convalescence. The vets had done a nice job on him. He didn't even limp, and he still doesn't, except when it rains hard for a couple of days. When he showed any sign of pain, I gave him a little whisky. When I got transferred to Japan, I bought Mike from the U.S. Army. Five dollars. He went everywhere with me. The Japanese thought he was a tame wolf. Nobody in Japan had ever seen a dog that weighed a hundred and twenty pounds. I used to have a problem finding food for him. You could give him five pounds of meat and he'd eat it before you could straighten up. He was expensive to feed. And he liked a little whisky every day.

"'One night I was in a bar, having a couple of beers and trying not to lose my temper with a big-mouth merchant seaman who was telling me how much he'd drunk one night in Marseilles and another night in Naples and so on. Finally I got fed up with him. I told him I had a dog that could drink more than he could.

"'That did it. First thing I knew there was a hundred dollars on the bar, and it was a case of put up or shut up. I didn't have the hundred, but I promoted it. When the sailor asked me what my hairy friend liked to drink, I decided I'd give old Mike whisky sours, for the energy in the sugar and the vitamins in the lemon juice. So the bartender made two whisky sours, we put Mike's in a rice bowl, he sniffed at it, stuck his tongue in, slurp, and that was that. The sailor drank his, and the bartender set 'em up again.

"'The sailor surrendered unconditionally at number twelve. I think he could have handled more, but he couldn't stay with Mike for speed. He couldn't stand the pace. Mike was *fast*. So we took the two hundred dollars and went looking for a butcher shop. That night we both had steak.

"'For the next six months Mike and I lived like kings—minor royalty, at any rate. Once a week—no oftener—Mike would accept a challenge. He never lost. We had some close squeaks, I must admit. There was an engineer off a Turkish freighter who almost did Mike in. He was a terror, that Turk. He caved in finally, though, like all the rest. I had to carry Mike home that night, but I was carrying five hundred dollars too.

"When I was discharged, the Army shipped Mike to Seattle for me. I gave one of the handlers three bottles of rye and told him that if he'd slip Mike a couple of shots a day, I'd buy him another three in Seattle, and I did. First, naturally, I went to see if Mike was looking cheerful and contented, which he wouldn't have been if the fellow had been holding out on him.

"'Well, all that was about nine years ago,' Jerry says, 'and Mike's not getting any younger. I've had some trouble with him, I just won't let him eat four or five pounds of meat at a sitting any more, and some-times he gets pretty sore at me. But it's when I cut down on his whisky that he gets *really* mad. He wants three ounces of toddy every night, and if he doesn't *get* three, there's trouble. I know he can count to three, and for all I know he can go to nine or ten. And if he sees me pour *two* drinks—well, a couple of times he's knocked the table over, and once he left the whisky in the dish and walked through the screen door without bothering to open it—things like that. One time he came over and leaned on me, he was so mad. He just leaned that hundred and twenty pounds on me and looked up as if to say that for two bits he'd take me out in the back yard and bury me for old bones.

"'So, lately,' Jerry says, 'I've been cutting his whisky half-and-half with water. I don't think he notices, just as long as he sees me pour three drinks. It's got to be done. Mike's just not as young as he used to be.'

"About two minutes later," Uncle Martin said, "there's an unholy banging and clattering on the door, and Jerry gets up to let this mon-ster in. He sits down beside the table, and Jerry says, 'I'll just give him a short one, so he can be sociable. He can't understand it if anybody else has a drink and he doesn't.' And he poured a small libation out of one

There is something truly irresistible about a German shepherd puppy. (Photograph © Barbara von Hoffmann)

of the cut bottles. It was a remarkable thing to see. The dog drank it nice and slow. He lapped up about half of it, and then he went over to his dish and had a little leftover meat, and then he came back and finished his drink. Remarkable animal."

"I should think so," I said. "I'm surprised he didn't challenge you to a contest."

"He was retired," Uncle Martin said. "And besides it wouldn't have been fair. Proportionately he was much older than I am. I'd have beat him for sure."

"I see," I said.

"Point is," Uncle Martin said, "you have to agree with me that Jerry Brainerd was watering that whisky for a good and even a noble cause."

"Right," I said.

"Which demonstrates that snap judgment is the foe of intelligence."

"Right," I said.

Uncle Martin held his glass to the light again. "No water in *this*," he said. "Have some."

"Tell me one more thing," I said. "This wonder dog, this hollow-leg terror—where does he live? I'd like to see him."

"Mike?" Uncle Martin said. "You're a little late. Mike is no longer with us."

"Just wouldn't learn to be moderate in his old age, I suppose?" I said.

"No," Uncle Martin said. "Wasn't that at all. An error in judgment his master made did Mike in. Both of them had developed a taste for Oriental food while they were in the service, and they used to go into New York and have a big dinner in Chinatown every couple of months—you know, the real thing, ten courses and all that, and none of this chop-suey nonsense. A few months ago they went in, but Jerry had picked the wrong day: It was the Chinese New Year. When Mike heard the first string of firecrackers go off, he ran amuck. He saw the Chinese fella who'd thrown them, and he jumped halfway across the street trying to get him. Car came along just then, and that was the end of old Mike. A soldier to the end, you might say."

"A very moving story," I said.

"There was an odd thing about it too," Uncle Martin said. "You know what the name of the fella driving the car turned out to be? Bourbon. Francis J. Bourbon. Came from New Jersey."

"A man given to snap judgments might find significance in that coincidence," I said. "As a matter of fact, it would be easy to form a snap judgment about the whole story."

"Avoid it," Uncle Martin said. "The snap judgment is the bane of the western world."

Facing page: Loyal not only to its owner, this shepherd carefully guards its red teddy bear. (Photograph © Marilyn "Angel" Wynn)

PART II

German Shepherds on the Job

"The German Shepherd Dog is first and foremost a working dog."
—*The Complete Dog Book,* 19th Edition, 1997

Above: *A K-9 cop with the Boise, Idaho, police department. (Photograph © William H. Mullins)*

Left: *A German shepherd keeps a wary eye on a flock of sheep. (Photograph © Tara Darling)*

The Phantom Car Gang

by Arthur Holman

For many who love German shepherds, the bond began with a utilitarian relationship. Breed guides often describe the shepherd as a worker that needs a task in life to be content. After all, German shepherds were originally bred to be working dogs—war dogs, Red Cross dogs, police dogs, sheep-herding dogs, and, later, Seeing Eye dogs. Close association between human and dog to achieve a goal that neither could accomplish alone leads to a mutual respect and a deep bond.

"The Phantom Car Gang" details a night in the life of police dog Rex III, a member of the Flying Squad of the London Metropolitan Police in the 1950s. The tale is spun by Rex's handler, Arthur Holman, and is excerpted from Holman's wonderful book, *My Dog Rex* (1957).

ᴄᴩ

Like Rex, this German shepherd with the Vorhees, New Jersey, police department is a powerful and relied-upon member of the force. (Photograph © Phil Marques)

THE NIGHT WAS bitterly cold, and the bombed house gave no protection from the icy November wind. I wanted desperately to stamp the numbness from my feet and breathe life into my fingers, but I dared not move for fear of revealing our presence. I longed for a cigarette and a hot drink, and found it hard to keep my eyes from the lighted windows of Maitland Court, with their infuriating suggestion of warm fires and slippered comfort.

At my feet, ears cocked, eyes hardly blinking, crouched [my German shepherd partner] Rex. He had sat there, uncomplaining and statue-still, for four shivering hours of unbroken monotony.

Slowly the minutes dragged by. My eyes ached as I stared into the deceptive shadows beyond the street lamps of Addison Road. . . .

There had been a smash-and-grab raid on a radio and television shop at Cricklewood. Although chased by a radio car, the gang, expertly driven in a Mark VII Jaguar, had escaped. Then came raids on a jeweller's in Regent Street and a radio shop at Fulham. The early editions of the evening papers were full of 'The Phantom Car Gang.'

On November 27, 1952, a few days after the Fulham raid, I came off duty to find a message telling me to ring Scotland Yard and speak to Superintendent Peck, the officer in charge of the dog section. 'Contact the Flying Squad,' he said. 'They want a dog to-night. The men we're after are known to be dangerous, and they're not afraid to use violence. They've said—and we believe them—that if a policeman tries to stop them they'll run him down.'

Information had reached the Yard that the Jaguar had been stolen from Piccadilly by a member of the gang dressed in chauffeur's uniform. The final numeral on its registration plates had been chipped off, changing the number from ALT 820 to ALT 82. The car was now kept in a lock-up at Maitland Court, a block of flats in Addison Road, Notting Hill, and although the woman who let the garage was quite innocent of any part in the affair, the gang set out from the lock-up on their raids, and returned to it with their loot. Requiring proof that they were more than car thieves, it was necessary for the Flying Squad to catch the gang red-handed. This meant long hours of watching and waiting, and Rex would be needed in case the crooks tried to run for it.

As I left the police station after my call to Peck I was smiling. This was the first time the Squad had asked for help from a dog, and it seemed to me that implicit in the choice of Rex was official acknowledgment that he was the finest dog attached to the Force.

At five that evening a Squad car picked me up at my home in Mitcham. We drove north-west to Notting Hill and cruised round to find the best observation-post. We selected the roofless, bombed house, and Rex and I climbed to its top storey. A whispered 'Sssh!' was enough for Rex to become motionless and silent, and our vigil began.

The versatile German shepherd is a working dog at its very foundation. (Photograph © Roxanne Kjarum)

After perhaps an hour I felt the first drops of rain. I hoped it was a light, passing shower, but the rain fell more and more heavily, until it was an icy, unbroken sheet. I turned up the collar of my mac and gave Rex a pat. He licked my hand as though to tell me he understood. The rain chilled my soul as well as my bones, and my clothes clung to me like cold, wet flannel. I prayed for some sort of action, and my heart leapt whenever I saw the rain-diffused glow of a car's lights. But no Jaguar either turned in at Maitland Court or drove out. The intervals between the mournful chimes of a neighbouring church clock seemed depressingly long.

Of 'The Phantom Car Gang' there was no sign, and at midnight it was decided that we should stand down. Delighted, but with no sign of cramp or stiffness, Rex jumped to his feet, shook himself, and bounded ahead of me down the stairs, tail wagging like a metronome. Inside the Squad car Rex curled up on the floor, and I sighed with pleasure at the thought of my bath and bed.

By the following evening rain had given way to frost. When we returned to the bombed house at six its torn floors were already carpeted with ice. Knowing now what was expected of him, Rex sat quietly at my side, revealing a patient tolerance that could have been equalled by few humans.

Again the agony of silent waiting—until 8:25, when we saw two men enter the lock-up in which we knew ALT 82 was garaged. A few minutes later the Jaguar came out, and there was no doubt that the man at the wheel was an expert driver. Leaving Rex, I ran down to confer with my colleagues—Detective-Sergeants Walters and Bridges and P.C. Donald Cameron. It was agreed that we could do nothing until the car returned, so I went back to my look-out post.

At 10:30, when the car drove back into the garage, I knew what to do. Followed by Rex, I hurried to the street. As I was in plain clothes, it would seem that I was a local resident taking my dog for a walk, and so I strolled slowly along Addison Road past Maitland Court. When I heard two men walk from the flats I hoped that the darkness would hide my tenseness as a reflex contracted my shoulder-blades. Then I heard the running feet of the C.I.D. men. The crooks hesitated for only a moment. One shouted, 'This way!' and they tore across the road and down a side-turning.

I spun round. Walters and Bridges had quickly caught up with one of the men, but the second, chased by Cameron, was leaving the policeman behind. 'Stop him!' I called—and Rex was away. Because of his training I did not need to tell him whom to stop. He ignored the two sergeants with their frantically struggling prisoner, overtook Cameron, and raced, greyhound-swift, after the criminal. I trotted behind, confident that Rex would catch, and hold, his man.

Hardly pausing in his stride, the crook scrambled over a six-foot gate. Undismayed, Rex jumped on to a wall alongside the gate. He skidded, rather than ran, along the narrow top of the gate—there was

Facing page: German shepherds are favored by the police because they are easy to train, strong, and have a deeply protective nature. The high breed recognition itself is a strong deterrent: Often a criminal suspect can be apprehended by fear of the dog alone. (Photograph © Tara Darling)

an eighteen-foot drop into an area had he fallen the wrong way—then disappeared between the houses. Thirty yards and a few seconds later it was over, with the suspect cornered against a dustbin and Rex holding the lapel of his coat vice-tight in his teeth.

'Leave,' I ordered. Rex released his grip, and ran round his prisoner, snarling with menace, teeth bared. I marched the man back to the gate and told him to climb over. I discovered then that Cameron, following me, had fallen down the area steps, injuring his arm. As Sergeant Walters came up the crook made a furious attempt at escape, and in the process of forcing him over the gate Walters fell, cracking a bone of his wrist.

Toughness is not a quality exclusive to criminals, and this one soon realized he was foolish to struggle. With Rex at our heels, we marched him back towards the garage, where Bridges was waiting with the other prisoner. The entire episode had taken no more than four minutes. But when we reached the street two more men came from the lock-up. They took one look at police and prisoners struggling in the road-way—and fled down Addison Road.

'Stop them!' I called, and again Rex showed his speed as the two fugitives disappeared into the darkness of Addison Road. He stopped the first man by leaping on his back and pushing him to the ground. He snapped at him, and the man lay still and started to cry. Rex hurtled after the second crook and seized his wrist in his teeth. Presently the four prisoners were lined up against a wall; guarding them, four police-men (two of us injured) and a dog.

We needed transport to take the men to the police station, so I said to Rex, 'Guard them,' and went to a near-by house, hoping the occu-pants had a telephone. But the door was opened by a boy of about eight and his baby sister. Surprisingly, they were alone in the house, and obviously terrified of the perspiring, panting, grimy stranger at the door. I tried to calm them, and explained that I was a policeman, but they were too scared to understand. I told them to go back to bed, and rejoined the others.

Walters went off to stop a car. As he hurried away one of the men suddenly dived across to a yard at the side of Maitland Court and clambered over a wall into the gardens beyond. I gave the order 'Stop him!' and Rex did not let me down. He disappeared over the wall in pursuit, and when I caught up with him he was standing over the sprawled body of the prisoner, teeth bared, and growling.

We halted a passing motorist, who dialled 999 for us, and ten minutes later we had the men safely inside Notting Hill Gate police station. In the back of the Jaguar we found a silver rose-bowl and two silver challenge cups worth £500: the gang had raided a hairdressing exhibition in Albemarle Street.

The leader of the gang was what we called, colloquially, 'a villain.' But he was a likable villain, and after he had been formally charged he said to me, 'No copper could catch me. It took a dog to do that. And if

With their particularly keen noses, shepherds are often employed to detect narcotics. Fire investigators even use the breed to sniff out fire accelerants at suspected arson scenes. (Photograph © David F. Clobes, Stock Photography)

you're going to use dogs regularly I'm going straight.' (Unfortunately he changed his mind, and it was Donald Cameron who again helped to arrest him in 1955, when he was given ten years for armed robbery, and for being concerned, with two other men, 'in shooting Detective-Sergeant Albert Eric John Chambers and Police-Constable Donald Cameron with intent to resist or prevent arrest.')

For his crimes with the 'Phantom Car Gang' he went to prison for four years, while his accomplices were sentenced to four years, two years, and eighteen months. And Rex? He received a commendation from the judge and an extra portion of liver from me.

First Lady of the Seeing Eye

by Morris Frank and Blake Clark

 Imagine what life was like for the blind before trained Seeing Eye dogs became available. Morris Frank knew well what it was like, having lost the sight in one eye at the age of six after an accident and the sight in the other eye at age sixteen after an errant boxing punch took him by surprise. In the world of the sightless in 1920s America, Frank had no choice but to hire a boy to help him find his way. But he longed for independence, and he found it through a German shepherd named Buddy.

"First Lady of the Seeing Eye" is the story of Frank's early experiences with Buddy, the first Seeing Eye dog in the United States. The idea of a dog leading around a blind person seemed incredible—even impossible and ridiculous—to most of that era, and Frank's story is truly a revolutionary tale; through Morris Frank's bravery and his later determination in forming the Seeing Eye, Inc., the world opened up for the blind in America.

This story is taken from the book by the same name, first published in 1957. Frank was assisted in writing by Blake Clark, author of several books and numerous articles for popular magazines.

ॐ

German shepherds are one of three breeds used as guide dogs for the blind; Labs and golden retrievers also fill the role. (Photograph © Isabelle Francais)

Perhaps the closest brush I have ever had with death came in a hotel corridor in Dayton, Ohio. The near-disaster occurred because I am blind. But it need not have happened at all; and it was solely my own fault.

I was scheduled to address a large convention in Dayton that evening, the train had arrived late and I was pressed for time. With Buddy, the Seeing Eye guide dog who served as my eyes, I rushed up to my room on the fourteenth floor. After I had freshened up I had only fifteen minutes to get to the convention hall. I had to hurry downstairs and find a cab.

With my ever-present German shepherd companion I hustled along the corridor to the elevator foyer. There Buddy stopped stock-still. She, who always walked up to an elevator and pointed with her nose to the call button for my convenience, would not approach this one. She ignored completely my "Forward" command. Then, in my great haste, I did what no Seeing Eye owner should ever do—I dropped the harness and started forward alone.

Buddy immediately threw herself across my legs, pushing so hard against me that I could not move ahead. At that moment a maid coming out of one of the rooms let out a terrified shriek.

"Don't move!" she shouted. "The elevator door's open, but the elevator's not there! There's only a hole!"

Morris Frank and Buddy. (Photograph courtesy of The Seeing Eye)

My knees all but buckled. Had Buddy let me take two more steps I would have disappeared down the empty shaft!

In that grateful and revealing instant there flashed through my mind an acute realization of just how much the loyalty and intelligence of that beautiful German shepherd lady had meant to me. And not only to me, but to all of the American blind who had secured freedom and independence through the use of trained guide dogs. For Buddy was the first Seeing Eye dog in America—the pioneer who opened the way for all the others. All her actions were attended by the widest publicity, and were watched with a curiosity which was at first profoundly skeptical. Had her performance not been brilliant and flawless, it is quite possible that the Seeing Eye program would never have got under way in America.

A few years earlier I had never heard of trained guide dogs for the blind. Then one day—I vividly remember the date, November 5, 1927—I was downtown in Nashville, Tennessee, where I was born and raised.

A brisk breeze laden with cold moisture from the Cumberland River chilled me as my attendant

A couple of pups—with ears akimbo—wait for dinner. (Photograph © Barbara von Hoffmann)

led me from my bank on Union Street. I pulled my topcoat collar up around my chin and then haltingly felt my way with my cane for the curb. I sensed my nearness to the corner newsstand. Charlie, the crippled vendor, shouted out to me, "Hey, Mr. Frank, there's a piece in this week's Post you oughta read! It's about blind folks like you."

I felt in my pocket for a nickel and handed it up. That five cents bought an article that was worth more than a million dollars to me. It changed my whole life.

That night—November 5, 1927—while I sat in the living room of our home on Richland Avenue, my father read those important words aloud. "This is called *The Seeing Eye,*" he began, his voice husky with emotion.

In the article, the author, Dorothy Harrison Eustis, described how the Germans had trained shepherd dogs to take the place of a blind man's eyes. I listened with mounting excitement as Father read that these marvelous dogs were equipped with a special harness, a firm, croquet-wicket-shaped leather handle that became a vital link between themselves and their masters. That short piece of leather was literally a lifeline. Through it the dog communicated as clearly and unhesitatingly as if he had been able to speak the words: "Straight ahead, path's clear"; "Slow down, sidewalk crowded"; or "Stop! Dangerous intersection!"

A dog would lead his charge at a fast walk so that any slackening of the gait could be instantly felt through the rigid handle. The miracle of it was that the animal could not only warn that the path ahead was not clear, he could even indicate what hazard was obstructing it. For curbs, be pulled back and stood still so his master could find the edge with his foot; for a bank of steps, he sat down; for busy traffic intersections, he "froze" until it was safe to cross. He swerved to either right or left to avoid stationary objects like scaffoldings and letter boxes, and he dodged oncoming pedestrians with uncanny agility.

As I listened, I could hardly control the wild hope that rose in me. If what we read about these wonder-working dogs was really true, they could free a person from the worst and most humiliating part of being blind—one's continual, helpless dependence on others. A companionable dog could take the place of an impatient human attendant, or— what was worse—a pitying one.

A dog's gentle pull could take me safely around open manholes, sidewalk-parked baby carriages, or the stray tricycles that were ever-present booby traps on even my simplest ventures outside the house. He could be my own personal red and green light at harrowing street crossings, sympathetically protecting me from potentially death-dealing tons of glass and steel on wheels.

My father paused in his reading. My mother, realizing what this revelation could mean to all of us, wordlessly sat down beside me. The promise held out seemed too good to be true.

The author herself told of her first skepticism. How could a dog be trained to do all that was claimed? An experience then at the Potsdam training school convinced her.

Facing page: *A four-month-old German shepherd posing in the snow. (Photograph © David F. Clobes, Stock Photography)*

She followed a blind man who set off with his guide dog, bound for the public gardens over a mile away. They safely negotiated city streets crowded with pedestrians. They crossed intersections alive with darting little automobiles, three-wheeled dog carts, and roaring motorcycles. So far, so good, but after all, the dog had successfully avoided only the *usual* type of hazard. Then the man and his four-footed guide approached one of those waist-high iron railings put up to keep cyclists off the sidewalk. Would the dog do the natural thing for her and simply trot on under the bar? If she did, the blind man would collide full force with the barrier for quite a blow right in his middle. Mrs. Eustis watched with a catch in her throat as she saw the dog, despite having to skirt a discarded coat on the ground, make for the narrow opening provided for pedestrians, and dog and master wheeled safely into the sunshine-filled, green park.

The future of all blind could be the same, the article promised. No longer dependent upon a member of the family, a friend, or a paid attendant, they could once more take up normal lives almost where they had been cut off. Each could begin or go back to a wage-earning occupation, secure in the knowledge that he could get to and from his work safely and without the cost of a hired guide; that crowds and traffic need no longer hold any terrors for him. His self-respect would be restored. After an honest day's work his evenings could be spent among friends without responsibility or burden to them; he need no longer be led home like a child—an ignominy that erased the whole pleasure of the visit.

"Gentlemen," the author concluded, "again without reservation, I give you the shepherd dog."

There was a choke in my father's voice as he finished. We sat silent for a moment, then all began talking at once. Our words overlapped, knocked into one another as flint against flint, ignited and lighted a once gloomy room with the blessed brightness of hope. After that evening, life was never the same for any of us.

I tossed and turned all night. One of these extraordinary animals could be the answer to my prayers. He could ease the bitterness I felt at losing my sight. By a series of coincidences—so rare that I wonder whether it ever happened to another family—my mother and I were both blinded accidentally, at times years apart, and each of us lost one eye at a time. Mother lost the first after a blood vessel in it burst while she was under strain of childbirth; a fall from a horse caused the loss of the second.

I lost my right eye at six when I ran into a tree limb while riding horseback. Then, at sixteen, came an unfortunate blow during a boxing match and within two days I saw no more. Now, after four years of blindness, the thought of the guide dogs opened vistas I had feared forever closed to me.

I visualized myself walking freely down the street. I would be able to make calls on prospective clients for my insurance business without the encumbrance of a talkative, incompatible guide. I could go to college on my own. I could even have a date—and it would not have to be a double date.

It meant that when I took a girl out, some other fellow would not take her up to her door and, for all I knew, get my good-night kiss. It would be me with my dog who would run up the front steps, tell my date good night, and come back to the car like a man.

Others who were handicapped could be men again, I thought, as I lay awake, impatient for the morning hours. There must be young men like me all over America who longed to break out of the prison of blindness. Those dogs would liberate us all.

The rising sun found me writing to Dorothy Harrison Eustis, in care of the *Saturday Evening Post*. My father typed as I dictated. "Is what you say really true?" I asked. "If so, I want one of those dogs! And I am not alone. Thousands of blind like me abhor being dependent on others. Help me and I will help them. Train me and I will bring back my dog and show people here how a blind man can be absolutely on his own. We can then set up an instruction center in this country to give all those here who want it a chance at a new life."

My hand trembled as I signed my name to this most significant letter of my life, then tapped my way to the mailbox near our home. I felt for the slot and dropped all my hopes down the narrow opening. The click of the lid signaled a new meaning to my life. It marked the

Amazingly, only an estimated 8,000 guide dog teams are in the United States and Canada today, though approximately 750,000 people are believed to be blind or visually impaired. (Photograph © Marilyn "Angel" Wynn)

start of a single motivating purpose that was to determine my every action for the next thirty years. At twenty I was a dedicated man.

Then began an agonizing period of waiting for a reply. I started to doubt what Mrs. Eustis had written. I must not let myself be carried away, I told myself. Maybe it was only magazine talk, sensationalism to sell an article. What if there aren't enough dogs to go around? What if the authorities would not let them come into this country? What if the dogs themselves could operate only in familiar German surroundings?

Questions, uncertainties, fears raced through my head. Anguish weighed me down. Was I destined to go on forever, step by timid step, tapping my way through life with a cane? For thirty agonizing days I went to our mailbox, looking in vain for Mrs. Eustis' answer to my plea.

The next morning I put off my trip to the mailbox, wanting to prolong the possibility of the letter's being there as long as I could. That was the time I should have raced to meet the postman. He had left a letter which I found out bore a bright blue and red Swiss stamp. From her home, "Fortunate Fields," near Vevey in the Swiss Alps had come the reply I had waited for so long. Father read it to me.

Mrs. Eustis explained that she was a Philadelphian, living in Switzerland. She loved dogs, and on her estate, Fortunate Fields, she trained German shepherds for use by the police, the Red Cross, and the Army.

She had never trained any guide dogs for the blind, she went on to say. At this my heart sank. It was a very highly special-

A pup sporting ears that would make your average mule jealous relaxes in a field of wildflowers. (Photograph © Barbara von Hoffmann)

Morris Frank and Buddy opened the world wide for so many. (Photograph © Barbara von Hoffmann)

ized job, she explained. However, she continued, if I really had the courage to come all the way from Tennessee to the mountains of Switzerland in search of a dog, she had a qualified trainer lined up for me.

My heart pounded as Father read on. Mrs. Eustis was coming to Philadelphia for Christmas and would telephone me at that time for my final decision.

Our family was in an uproar. Father was all for my going. He wanted to take me himself, but could not leave his business. Mother had serious misgivings about the long journey. Some friends said, "You're crazy, chasing all the way across the ocean after a dog." Others said, "Morris, it sounds great. What can you lose?"

For an expert opinion I wrote to Dr. Edward E. Allen, a personal friend and director of the Perkins Institute for the Blind. "You have a long life ahead of you," he wrote me. "You have always rebelled against being dependent upon other people. Perhaps this will solve your problem—and not only yours but, if your plan goes through, that of thousands more just like you. You are young, boy. Take a chance, not only for yourself but for others." After this Mother agreed to let me undertake the voyage.

Two weeks later I received a telegram from Mrs. Eustis saying she would telephone that night. Excitement was intense at home as the hour drew near. I took my place by the phone and waited nervously. When it finally rang, I jumped with surprise. Then I heard a quiet, cultivated voice, "Mr. Frank, do you still think you want to come to Switzerland for your dog?"

I could not answer; I was too choked up. That heavenly voice went on, warningly yet encouragingly, "It's a very long trip for a blind boy alone."

"Mrs. Eustis," I fairly shouted, regaining my voice, "to get back my independence, I'd go to hell!"

I went to Switzerland in April as if I were a parcel—by American Express. The experience angered and frustrated me and made me all the more determined to undergo any hardship to overcome dependency on others.

I was put in the charge of a particularly unimaginative steward. Rather than being an attendant, he was more of a jailer in ship's clothing. Each morning I was a prisoner in my locked-from-the-outside cabin until he came to escort me to breakfast. As soon as I finished my coffee, he led me back to my quarters.

At ten he exercised me as if I were a horse, methodically trotting me around the deck. Then he deposited me in a steamer chair. If some friendly passenger invited me to take a stroll, we got only a few feet before my keeper ran up breathless, grasped my elbow, and steered me to my seat again where be could keep an eye on me.

I met a delightful English girl with whom I wanted to be alone in the evening. But we could not escape that sleuthing steward. No matter whether we tried to enjoy the shadows cast by a friendly upper-deck lifeboat or took a remote corner of the ship's lounge, come nine o'clock that pest ferreted us out, took me in tow, and locked me in my cabin for the night. American Express and the captain of that ship certainly took seriously their responsibility to the blind man aboard!

"I'll make up for this," I thought grimly, "when they turn me loose in Paris."

Paris! I could hardly wait to get to that city that holds so many treasures of the past and pleasures of the present. I yearned to make my way along the grand boulevards. I wanted to hear the lapping of the Seine against the ancient bridges. The Emperor Napoleon had always been my favorite character of history; I intended to visit his tomb at the Invalides and run my hands over the marble mausoleum in which he lies sleeping.

I looked forward to a stop at a sidewalk café. There I would sip an *apéritif*, listen to the laughter of Métro-bound shopgirls, and overhear the exotic accents of my fellow revelers from all over the world. To me, even the shrill horns of the passing taxicabs were going to be a thrill. Though blind, I meant to savor the delights of the queen of cities.

I got off the boat train at the Gare du Nord and was left alone for what seemed hours and hours.

"Mr. Frank?" finally came the brisk inquiry in a woman's voice with a Parisian accent. It was the representative from American Express.

"You are to come with me, please," she said in a cold, businesslike tone I never thought could belong to a Frenchwoman.

She took me to a little hotel and up to a musty-smelling room.

"A bottle of wine and some biscuits are on the table," she said as she slammed the door behind her.

I felt my way to the bottle and had a glass of wine. Then I groped for the telephone to order some food; I was ravished with hunger. No one spoke English, and I knew no French. I felt my way around the wall to the door—the last ignominy—she had locked it!

In desperation I finished the bottle and crackers and fell asleep. Hours later someone rudely shook me awake.

"Get up, Mr. Frank. It's midnight. Time to go to your train."

It was the woman from American Express. My stay in Europe's loveliest city had come to an end.

I stepped down from my train compartment into the warm sunshine and the fresh cool air of spring in Vevey, Switzerland.

"Mr. Frank, here we are!" were the first welcome words I heard. It was Mrs. Eustis' lovely voice. She shook my hand warmly.

"With me are our director of training and genetics, Jack Humphrey, Mrs. Humphrey, and their little George, who's four," she said, and we shook hands cordially all around.

Mrs. Eustis, this friendly person who had already become such an important part of my life, was small, about five feet two, I judged. By the way she spoke to her chauffeur and the others, she impressed me as being considerate yet firm, one who had high standards of conduct for herself and for others. I could tell she was one who knew how to get what she wanted—a good person to take up one's cause. I sat between her and gentle Mrs. Humphrey on the drive up the narrow, winding roads of Mount Pelerin to the gates of Fortunate Fields.

I was a little bewildered as they described the new world I was entering. The chalet was most impressive, consisting of two spacious connecting buildings, one of three stories, the other rising to four!

We left our hats and coats in a small anteroom, its floor paved by stones worn smooth during generations of use. It opened into a long parlor with a billiard table in the center. At the far end comfortable chairs were set before a fireplace that sent out a cozy warmth and pleasant crackling.

I memorized the layout of my immediate surroundings, using the game room as my starting point. To my left a door opened to Mrs. Eustis' suite. On the right I would have to watch out for the stairway that led up to the dining room. Straight ahead lay a real hazard—a short flight of three steps leading down to a tremendous living room. In one vaulted corner stood a priceless grand piano that belonged to Josef Hofmann, former owner of Fortunate Fields. As I stood beside it, they told me that the room gave on a magnificent view that soared beyond the Swiss border to the mountains of Italy and France. Little George shoved into my hand a picture he had drawn and shyly said, "It's of what you could see, if you could see, out the window!"

After dinner Jack Humphrey told me something about their work. Mrs. Eustis was interested chiefly in breeding a strain of German shepherds with high teachability. To prove them, she trained them for sentry and police duty and rescue work.

Facing page: *The extraordinarily versatile German shepherd not only has served as a guide dog to the blind, but has delivered messages on wartime fronts, helped rescuers find victims after bombings or avalanches, led U.S. Customs agents to hidden caches of narcotics, apprehended just about every kind of fugitive imaginable, and provided much needed therapy to those feeling blue. (Photograph © Barbara von Hoffmann)*

Jack was to be my instructor. He had spent a month of highly specialized work in Potsdam to learn the technique. First he had concentrated on the training of guide dogs. That mastered, he studied ways of teaching the blind to use them. I was to be his first pupil. Tomorrow, he said, he would introduce me to my dog, a German shepherd that had been specially selected from the finest of her breed. The day after, we would begin training.

I spent the next morning torn between impatience and nervousness. What would this new animal in my life be like? Would she like me? I knew she was handsome. Mrs. Eustis had described her as a beautiful dark gray with a creamy patch at her throat. Her sensitive ears were always alert, her soft brown eyes brilliant and full of understanding. How I hoped I'd look as good to her as, in my mind's eye, she already did to me.

It was not until afternoon that Jack said, "Morris, I'll bring your dog."

My dog!

"Here's something to give her," he said, putting a small ball of ground meat into my hand. "You must start winning her affection."

He left but in a few minutes returned. I heard the door open and the soft fall of the dog's paws on the floor. I held out the morsel and while she accepted it with dignity, I knelt and patted her, stroking her soft, silky coat.

How lovely she was! And it was in her power to deliver to me the divine gift of freedom! I felt a surge of affection for her.

Jack stood by quietly. "What's her name?" I asked him.

"Kiss," he answered.

"Kiss!" I exclaimed. My face turned red as I pictured my embarrassment at calling out, "Here, Kiss! Come, Kiss!" in a crowd of strangers. "That's a hell of a name for a dog," I told him brusquely. Then I put my arms around my new friend and told her, "I'm going to call you Buddy."

I took Buddy's leash and made a fuss over her all afternoon. Already attached to her trainers and fond of her playmates in the kennel, she merely tolerated me. She was pleased that night, however, to be taken to sleep beside my bed in my warm room, instead of to the dogs' quarters.

Cold air racing off the snow-capped mountains next morning caused me to snuggle down under the blankets and resist coming to consciousness. Then a warm tongue licked my face. I remembered I was in Switzerland, on top of Mount Pelerin, and this was Buddy. All that had happened to me in the past few weeks had not been a dream.

I got up, dressed, and took Buddy down the outside stairs to the yard to take care of her morning needs. We then proceeded to the dining room, where the family had gathered at the breakfast table by the bay window overlooking Lake Léman. After delicious wild strawberries with rich Alpine cream and strong black coffee Jack pushed his

Facing page: *Lovably awkward and goofy, German shepherd pups will latch on tight to the heart of just about anyone. (Photograph © Sharon Eide/Elizabeth Flynn)*

One of the reasons German shepherds make such excellent guide dogs for the blind is that they are supremely smart dogs that can be easily trained to do what is needed. (Photograph © Marilyn "Angel" Wynn)

chair back and said, "Well, it's time to go to work, Morris."

At last my training was to begin. I went back to my room, buckled on Buddy's harness, and met Jack at the front door.

"Pick up your handle in your left hand—the dog always works on your left side, between you and pedestrian traffic," Jack said in a quiet, firm voice. "Keep your shoulders back and walk with the stride of a soldier.

"Now give the command 'Forward' and give it clearly. As soon as the dog responds, reward her with praise."

I took the harness, my heart pounding, and said, somewhat shakily, "Forward!" Then, "That's a good girl!" The handle almost jerked out of my hand, and we simply flew to the gate. Buddy stopped before it, and for a moment I teetered back and forth and almost lost my balance.

"She's showing you where the latch is," said Jack.

I put my hand on her head, slid it down her nose, and found she could not have indicated the location of the latch more accurately if she had been a teacher with a wooden pointer. I lofted it and we started through.

"Keep your free arm close to your side or you'll hit the gate post," warned Jack.

Following Jack's instructions, I gave the commands "Right" and "Forward"—this time a little less timidly—and down the road we went at a clip I had not gone in years. I heard, "Keep your shoulders back."

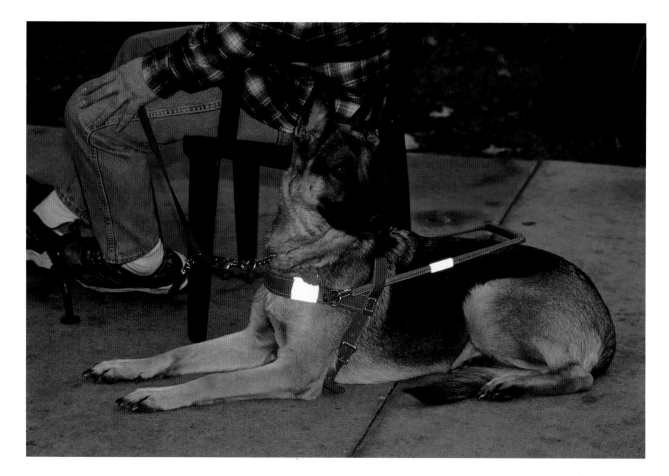

As I straightened, I unconsciously threw out my chest. My stride lengthened and I heard Mrs. Eustis' voice saying, "Look, his head has gone up!"

No wonder! It was glorious—just a dog and a leather strap linking me to life. We were bound for Vevey—a funicular ride away and down the mountain side from Fortunate Fields. I was keenly aware of the people, the dog carts, the push carts, the horses and wagons on the sloping road leading to the small depot. As I was visualizing the jostle and enjoying the crisp air, Buddy abruptly stopped. "Ah, the funicular steps, probably," I thought, and slid my foot forward. Sure enough, there was a low platform! How exciting! "Forward! That's a good girl!" I cried. I felt Buddy's harness tilt, giving me a gentle pull, and up we went.

Jack sat with us when we found places on the cable car.

"Put the dog under your knees so no one steps on her," he said. I felt the jerking start of the tension-controlled car, and twenty minutes later we had grated our way down the hill to the center of the little city.

My first blurred memory of Vevey is a mélange of commands and swift, exhilarating walk, of the sound of the clopping of horses' hoofs on stone streets and the chatter of people whose language I could not understand. Then more stops, more commands, and more curbs.

On a narrow sidewalk the feel of the harness told me Buddy was swerving to the right, and I swerved with her. "She just took you around a man carrying two big bushel baskets of beans," said Jack.

Buddy stopped. I pushed my foot forward but felt nothing. Jack laughed. "It's not a step," he explained. "A woman stopped in front of you. Give Buddy the 'Forward' command."

I did, and we skirted the obstacle. "That mother was blocking the way with a baby carriage and Buddy had to wait for her to move her youngster before we could get by," Jack said.

At one point Buddy deftly swung out to the left, then back in line again. I felt no presence of person or building nearby. "Why did she do that?" I asked Jack.

"Put your hand up," was his reply.

I did, and at about eye level hit an iron pipe, the framework support of an awning. It would have struck me right in the face but for Buddy. This, to me, seemed the most amazing guiding she had done. Traveling alone, she would hardly have noticed that heavy structure, so far above her, but with me in tow, her eyes had measured it against my six feet. She had received no command, she acted entirely on her own responsibility. When she did that, she was thinking! Hers were, indeed, my seeing eyes. *"That's a good girl!"* I said with feeling.

Each new experience gave me more the feel of the harness, the ability to relax, and increased my trust in Buddy. For two hours Jack constantly interpreted the movements of my dog and reminded me to walk erectly and not grip the lead-rein too tightly. Buddy worked with a gay air, tail wagging, as though she enjoyed knowing so much more than I did.

It was so exciting that not until I reached home and sank into a comfortable chair did I realize how exhausted I was. My feet hurt, the muscles of my legs ached from the unaccustomed exercise, my left arm was sore and my back hurt from pulling against the harness. But these aches added up to the best feeling I had had in years.

After we had taken a morning and an afternoon excursion each day for five days, Jack said, "Tomorrow, you're on your own. I'll follow at some distance behind you, but I won't interfere."

I trembled inwardly. With every trip Jack had become more strict. He did not tolerate mind-wandering. If I was carried away by the exhilaration of a brisk walk, he would bring me back to earth with a gruff prompting that I was in training. He was an excellent coach.

"You'll get no more reminders," he warned. "If you don't do what I've tried to teach you, you may get a good bump. That'll penetrate that thick skull of yours!"

I listened, thinking hopefully, "He wouldn't dare let me get hurt."

When Buddy and I appeared at the front door next morning, Jack carefully reviewed for me every turn and block of the route to the city and back. Then, for the first time, we set out on our own.

At the gate, instead of stopping immediately when Buddy did, I took two steps and ran smack into the post. There was Jack's big laugh behind me and a hearty, "I told you, but you wouldn't listen."

Long-haired German shepherds are not favored by those involved with dog shows; for everyone else, a shaggy German shepherd is just as wonderful as a more close-cropped dog. (Photograph © Marilyn "Angel" Wynn)

I lifted the latch, pretending I had done nothing more than brush the gate post, and laughed back.

"Forward and right," I commanded. Buddy did not move. Jack said not a word. "Oh, I mean—right, forward!" I corrected myself, disconcerted to have made two errors in about two minutes. I felt Buddy's tail wag, and on our way we went.

Buddy paused as usual at the steps to the funicular, but I was

nervous and did not halt myself promptly. I stumbled and fell down, giving my knees a good thwacking. Jack did not even say, "Did you hurt yourself?" He just laughed. Brushing off the dust, I clenched my teeth and thought, "That's a mean way to treat a blind man."

I took a seat in the cable car and, immersed in my own chagrin, allowed Buddy to flop down in front of me without seeing to it that her feet were well out of people's way. Jack purposely stepped on her paw and she yelped. I hastily put her under my knees as I was supposed to do and sat there, a very dejected fellow. That cable car did not plummet any faster downhill than did my own spirits.

Jack did not speak to us. "Why does he laugh at me like that?" I thought, resentfully. "Why didn't he save me from falling? And why did he feel it was necessary to step on my dog just to teach me a lesson?"

In Vevey, feeling discouraged and still angry at Jack, I followed Buddy lackadaisically, although she was moving with alacrity. My shoulder grazed several people, a forceful and humiliating reminder to bring my arm in closer to my side.

By the time we reached our first corner, I was in a boiling rage and did not listen for the sound of traffic, as Jack had instructed. Rashly I gave my command, "Forward." Halfway across, Buddy made an abrupt stop, then hurriedly backed up, dragging me with her. I felt a car zoom past, so close that its rear wheels threw stinging gravel in my face. That brought me to my senses. When we reached the safety of the opposite curb, I gave her a big, heartfelt hug.

On the return trip to Fortunate Fields I did better. I relaxed more and followed my guide with an easier gait. But I had not relaxed my attitude toward Jack.

"I don't want any lunch," I said when we got back to the house, and went right on up to my room.

I was lying on the bed telling Buddy how unfairly I was being treated when I heard the door open and someone enter.

"Look, boy"—it was Jack's voice. "You have your choice: you can be just another blind man or you can be a man on your own with Buddy's eyes to help you. You can't lean on me. If I have to follow you and tell you everything, you aren't going to depend on your dog. You won't be able to master the signals."

I didn't answer.

"When you go back to the United States," Jack continued, "I won't be there. Your future's up to you."

He had quietly closed the door before I realized he was gone. I was ashamed. Jack wasn't unsympathetic, I told myself. He was absolutely right.

That night I went to bed feeling lonely and discouraged. What if I couldn't learn to use a guide dog, after all? What if my concentration was too poor? What if I couldn't communicate with Buddy? What a fool I'd feel returning to Nashville and admitting I'd been a failure. Other blind I wanted to help would never even know I'd tried.

Facing page: *A white German shepherd pup. (Photograph © Sharon Eide/Elizabeth Flynn)*

A shepherd in late afternoon light. (Photograph © Isabelle Francais)

It came over me with a rush that I was a far piece from home; an ocean and a foreign country separated me from those who loved me. For the first time I felt really homesick.

Then, as if she knew how low-spirited I was, Buddy got up from her place by my bed. She crawled up on top of the covers beside me, nuzzled the back of my neck, and snuggled as close to me as she could, giving a long low grunt of contentment and companionship.

Her warm affection completely changed my mental attitude. In reviewing the morning, I thought it had not been so bad, really. I had made mistakes, but I had learned a lot from them. I had done fairly well on the last part of the trip. Even Jack had said that was so. "A pretty good job," he'd told me, "for your first run without help."

Most important, Buddy had shown me that if I did my part, we two would walk together in safety. My heartache gone, I dropped off to sleep with the comfort of Buddy close beside me.

That night a partnership was born, the beginning of a life together—a man and a dog, a man whose dog meant to him emancipation, a new world, and other worlds to conquer.

Our training trips became more difficult. Jack mapped out trial runs for Buddy and me that forced us to learn to move together under all conditions. One day we had an unexpected test of our responses. As we trudged up the narrow way from the cable car, my ears were assailed by a heavy rumble and a wild clatter of staccato hoofbeats.

"Runaway horses!" I thought as the turmoil bore down upon us. I was helpless to know which way to turn to escape. But not Buddy! She lunged to the right, off the side of the road, with such force she almost jerked me off my feet. Then the harness handle tilted until I was reaching up over my head to maintain my grasp, and she had me stumbling up a steep embankment. She literally hauled me up the seven-foot rocky slope. We stopped, panting, at the top—out of the way just in time as the team of snorting, mad animals careened past, dragging a hurtling, crashing wagon.

When it was all over and I had come down and patted and praised Buddy, I suddenly realized that Jack had seen the whole episode. Too far behind to help, he had simply held his breath and prayed that we would survive the emergency. Thanks to Buddy, we did.

As the lessons progressed, my powers of concentration increased so that when listening to directions I never had to ask that they be repeated. I gave my commands in a loud, clear voice, aimed straight at the back of Buddy's head; my vocal chords grew stronger. I became more sensitive to Buddy's communications. I could even tell if she moved her head to the left or right.

Jack now trusted us to find our way about Vevey without his following close behind. After accompanying us down the hill in the cable car, he would send us off on our own. We became a familiar duo on the little city's cobblestone streets, and received many greetings. By now I could recognize and reply to the individual *"Bonjours!"* of the postman, the flower lady, and the underworked *gendarme*.

Buddy and I sped swiftly about on the itineraries Jack laid out for us. He and I customarily had a glass of beer at the depot's sidewalk café if I got back before the cable car arrived. It didn't take long until I was making Jack's mapped-out tours in time to have two beers before the car came. This, I thought, was worthwhile progress.

I typed happy letters to my mother and father: "Think of it—being able to go where I please. You know I haven't wept in four years, but when that dog pilots me safely across the street with automobiles whizzing past all around us, I just feel like sitting down on the pavement, throwing my arms around her neck, and crying." When I thought that all the blind in America might have this same kind of protective companionship, my exhilaration was multiplied a thousandfold.

But it was not all beer and skittles. One day I stopped at a Vevey crossing with Buddy and felt an authoritative tug at my coat sleeve. A lady with a clipped British accent then told me, "Young man, it's an outrageous thing to put a poor dog into slavery!"

"Ma'am," I said, patiently, "this dog knows she is loved, belongs, and is needed. She's not turned out in the morning when children go to school and left to fend for herself until they get back in the afternoon. Nobody throws rocks at her, and her water pan is not left dirty or empty. When this dog is hungry, she doesn't have to turn over a garbage pail."

A disapproving silence told me it would take some talking to convince this woman.

"What a dog wants more than anything else is human companionship," I went on. "In return for the love and affection I give her and for keeping her well groomed and clean and cared for, she gladly serves as my eyes."

My lecture not only failed to persuade her; it made her irate.

"My good fellow," she said, and I pictured her clenching her teeth and shaking an umbrella, "if you came all this way from the United States, you must have money. Why don't you hire somebody there to take care of you and lead you about? Why do you have to come over here and enslave a poor foreign dog?"

And, to clinch her argument, she demanded, bitingly, "Aren't you a Christian?"

With that, I tipped my hat and said, "No, Ma'am, I am a Mohammedan! Buddy, forward!"

One other encounter with an Englishwoman left me feeling rather sorry for the lady.

"When will your dog have puppies?" she asked.

I explained that Buddy was a career girl, destined never to become a mother.

"Oh, dear, the poor thing," she murmured sympathetically. "She'll always be an old maid, just like me!"

I had been at Fortunate Fields several weeks when one morning I said to Mrs. Eustis, "I'd like to get a haircut. I guess I'll ask Jack to take me to the barber shop."

"Take yourself," she answered. "You have your dog."

What a challenge! I had never made the round trip to the city—portal to portal—alone all the way. My hands became moist and I felt warm all over with excitement. It would be the first time I dared set out on my own initiative, without leaning on Jack.

"Forward, Buddy!" my voice rang out.

My senses seemed sharpened as she and I followed the familiar pattern of paths that led from gate to funicular and to Vevey itself.

Now I repeated over and over to myself the directions I had been given. I felt like a child trying to find his way through a maze—only this wasn't a game, this was in earnest. What if I got hopelessly lost? What if I failed to find the barber and had to return home, not only shaggy thatched but a failure as well?

I counted the curbs as we passed by the village shops. The clucking of hens told me I had arrived at the poultryman's corner. I turned left. Soon I smelled the fragrance from the crusty loaves at the bakery and I was reassured that we were on the right track.

"Right, Buddy," I said.

Then, suddenly, borne on the heavenly scent of bay rum, I heard the barber's cheery "Good morning, Monsieur!"

Morris Frank went on to become a successful insurance salesman. Here he is walking with his third Seeing Eye dog, Buddy III, in the 1950s. (Photograph courtesy of The Seeing Eye)

I'm sure that man never had a more enthusiastic, happy response to any greeting he had ever tendered in his long career of scissors-wielding!

My haircut pleased me as much as if it had been specially designed and executed for me by the famous hairdresser at the Ritz, and my pal Buddy and I made the trip home as if on wings, rather than propelled by our combined six feet.

I sat down in the living room, threw back my head and laughed, roared until the tears came to my eyes.

"What's got into you, Morris?" asked Mrs. Eustis.

A German shepherd pauses for a drink from a mountain stream. (Photograph © Alan and Sandy Carey)

"Ma'am," I said, "I've been blind since I was sixteen. For years someone has had to take me to the barber shop. I've been left waiting there like unclaimed luggage for hours at a time. Sometimes my father would deposit me on his way to work at nine and I would have to sit there until he came back to pick me up at noon. Today when I mentioned a haircut to you, you told me where to go for it and how to get there. I took my dog, or rather, my dog took me, I got my own haircut and came back. Now for the first time I'm convinced that I am really going to be free. That's why I'm laughing—because I'm free, by God, I'm free!"

No sighted person could ever understand the magnitude of my relief. I felt like a bound eagle that had been loosed to soar again. I had maintained a smile on my face since I was a teen-ager, to keep up a front. This was my first genuine laugh in four years.

As the time drew near for me to "graduate" and go back home, Mrs. Eustis, Jack, and I had long conferences about my plans for an organization to bring Buddies to the blind in America. Where would we begin? Who could provide the money? Could we find a sufficient number of intelligent dogs in the U.S.? Who there could train them and teach the blind to use them?

We thought it might be best to plan to begin with an office in Nashville, since that was my home and it was also fairly centrally located. We could branch out from there. It would be ideal if we could get help from already established charitable agencies for the blind. Many strategically situated throughout the various regions of the country already had housing accommodations, grounds—and money to spend on rehabilitation. If they would join us with such facilities and financial aid, we could start almost immediately. We could begin right away to train as many of the blind as available dogs and instructors would permit. Failing agency cooperation, depending on our own limited funds, we would have to start on a very modest scale indeed.

Fortunate Fields could supply a few dogs and trainers in the beginning. If things went well, the entire staff and kennels could, if necessary, be converted to helping supply the needs of the new enterprise.

"All this is looking far ahead," said Mrs. Eustis. "Whether any school for guide dogs can ever get started at all depends upon two things very close at hand. Number one, although we here are confident that Buddy can give you complete freedom of movement, few people at home will believe it. And even we cannot say for certain how a dog trained here in little Vevey will perform in the unfamiliar, perhaps confusing, conditions of U.S. metropolitan areas. You and Buddy will have to go from city to city and prove beyond the shadow of a doubt that it is not only possible for you to get about but that it is practically as easy for you as for any sighted person."

That was, indeed, a large order. I shuddered as I visualized the traffic bedlam of Chicago's "Loop."

"Number two," Mrs. Eustis continued, "you must not forget that signs saying 'No Dogs Allowed' are almost everywhere—in restaurants, hotels, office buildings, and stores. If the blind man's dog can't be with him in the places he has to go, of what value is it to him? And what about restrictions on trains, streetcars, and busses? If a person can't use his dog to get to work, it's obvious he can't hold down a job. How will it ever be possible for the organization to succeed unless the guide dogs are welcome in all public places?"

It was a sobering thought.

"So, your second task," she concluded, "is to get Buddy accepted all over America with no more fuss than if she were a cane."

This would be far from easy. It would take phenomenal effort before Buddy would be permitted even to stick her cold nose into many establishments I could think of. Once she was in them, only a very convincing demonstration of good conduct could persuade those in charge to relax rules of many years' standing.

"On my last trip to the States," Mrs. Eustis went on, "I remember seeing some blind beggars on the streets with dogs as companions. The thought of those defeated-looking tin cups still makes me cringe. You, Morris, must set a new picture in the public mind. You must hold your head high and make a blind man and his dog now stand for dignity and self-reliance."

Doubts assailed me. Was I taking on an assignment that I would never be able to carry out?

"Of course this last part of your groundwork will require some long spadings," said Mrs. Eustis, as if reading my thoughts. "It takes time

The German shepherd is one of the smartest, easiest to train, and most loyal dogs, but sometimes a goofy gene slips into the genetic soup. (Photograph © Roxanne Kjarum)

to break down prejudice. But you can judge Buddy's prowess in strange traffic by the time you get back to Nashville. Stop over in every large city on the way and put her to the acid test in every one of them. Don't spare her. If you and she meet the challenge and prove that the blind and their dogs can successfully negotiate the traffic of America's city streets, I will guarantee ten thousand dollars and send a staff to help you start the guide dog school."

We talked about a name for my proposed organization.

"I'd like to call it 'The Seeing Eye,'" I told Mrs. Eustis, "The title of the article that brought us together."

"I think that would be very appropriate, Morris," she answered. "It's from a Book that has been an unsurpassed guide itself for centuries: Proverbs 20:12, 'The hearing ear, and the seeing eye, the Lord hath made even both of them.'"

When it was time for *"au revoir,"* Mrs. Eustis, Jack, Mrs. Humphrey, and little George drove Buddy and me to the station, and they wished us Godspeed.

"Morris, you're a far cry from the timid, stooped, uncertain boy we met here less than six weeks ago," said Mrs. Eustis as she pressed my hand in farewell. "We're *so* proud of you!"

I had no words with which to thank her. My heart was too full. I would always be grateful to all of them. They would never know—I myself could hardly tell—what the days had done for me. Fortunate Fields were aptly named, I thought. They had restored my self-confidence.

I pulled my shoulders back, I took a deep breath, threw out my chest, and stood as tall as I could. I felt ready for the tremendous job ahead: to try to make it possible for my fellow American blind to sign their Declaration of Independence.

With tongue lolling, a German shepherd stops for a portrait on an urban footbridge. (Photograph © Isabelle Francais)

PART III

The Idiosyncratic Shepherd

"As a rule, [my German shepherd] the Duchess is benevolent in manner, but at the faint distant sound of an approaching speedboat, she becomes a fair imitation of the Hound of the Baskervilles. Her hackles rise and her eyes glow like coals in the grate. From the nearest point on the shore she bays defiance at each of these passing demons and, as it goes roaring on its way, returns to the house, smug in her conviction that she's driven it off. . . . To the boat she seems to be three hounds of the Baskervilles—enough to start the useful myth that we are protected by a pack of ferocious bloodhounds."
—Alexander Woollcott, radio broadcast, 1939

Above: *Six-week-old littermates make a particularly impressive performance in abject cuteness. (Photograph © Marilyn "Angel" Wynn)*

Left: *An adolescent German shepherd wades in Idaho's Stanley Lake. (Photograph © Jeff and Alexa Henry)*

My Friend Egon

by Alexander Woollcott

The nature of a German shepherd is distinctive, an intriguing blend of fierce loyalty, supreme intelligence, and a zest for life. These hallmarks of the breed are at the heart of the German shepherd's popularity.

Like Brooks Atkinson whose work also appears in this anthology, Alexander Woollcott is best known as a drama critic. He worked for several New York newspapers, including the *Times,* the *Herald,* and the *World,* wielding a great deal of power over the fate of plays on the New York stage. He later became a full-time freelance writer, penning several books, editing numerous anthologies, collaborating on two plays, and writing a regular column for the *New Yorker.*

"My Friend Egon" first appeared in the book *Two Gentleman and a Lady* (1928).

The quizzical look and draping tongue of a young shepherd. (Photograph © Norvia Behling)

IF BY ANY chance, you spent the summer of 1928 at Antibes, you need no introduction to my friend Egon. You could scarcely have missed him, even though that once slumbrous cape has, of late years, been aswarm with the conspicuous. Probably the manager of the Hotel du Cap himself could not tell you why, in obedience to the ever reliable herd instinct of the human species, the drift of the summer tourists turned, a few seasons after the war, toward his deserted corner of the Riviera. He merely thanks God and rubs his hands.

In the crowd, you must have seen Lloyd Osborne, indistinguishable from a lizard on the sun-baked rocks in front of his terra cotta home. You may have seen Mary Garden or Lily Langtry, perhaps, running over from Monte Carlo to a dinner party at the Cap. You can hardly have escaped the Dwight Deere Wimans (late of Moline, Ill.) and the Archibald MacLeishes and the Charles Bracketts (late of Saratoga), taking up an unconscionable part of the *plage* with their respective young. You doubtless saw Mrs. James Hazen Hyde, bearing up with remarkable fortitude under the continual annoyance of being mistaken for Marie Tempest. And perhaps you even saw Marie Tempest herself. Or Elsie deWolfe (Lady Mendl, to you) throning away in La Garoupe, the largest villa at the Cap. Oh, these, and Montemezzi, perhaps, and Moronzoni, and Walker Ellis of New Orleans, and Benjamin Strong of the Federal Reserve Bank, and (so as to have a little of everything) Dudley Field Malone.

But it is none of these you will remember longest. The unforgettable habitué of Antibes is Egon. He had been wintering and springing in New York, and you might have seen him almost any day that you dropped in at the White Horse Tavern in West 45th Street, where he rather made a point of keeping an eye on the coatroom, being, I think, the only coatroom attendant in town who could dispose of a troublesome customer, or even knock off for the day, merely by executing a neat standing broad jump over the counter. But with the coming of spring to West 45th Street, Egon began to betray a nostalgia for Antibes and made it clear enough that he was obliged to meet a friend over there. Victorio, the coatroom boy at the Algonquin, had left in April for six months of painting in Paris. I shouldn't be at all surprised if Egon got the idea from him.

At that time, Egon still belonged to the younger generation, having been born as recently as 1921. He is one of the largest and most powerful German police dogs ever bred in the kennels of Berlin. Even, when he was very young, he cost as much as a high powered automobile. He was acquired when he was a yearling by Benjamin Ficklin Finney, Jr., sometime student in residence at the University of Virginia and later a Captain in the United States Marines in France where, I need hardly add, he was popularly known as Finney la Guerre.

Benjamin Ficklin Finney, Sr., stays the year round in Sewanee, Tenn., where he is the Regent of the University of the South. Benjamin Ficklin Finney, Jr., having inherited the famous Penelo Plantation

Facing page: Curiosity is a common trait in German shepherds, but this shepherd seems quite uninterested in an equestrian friend. (Photograph © Kent and Donna Dannen)

at Tarboro, N. C., stays nowhere at all very long and, to put it in a nutshell, does nothing in particular. But, like the House of Lords, he does it very well.

When last heard from in December of 1927, Massa Ben, as the old planter is sometimes called, was on his way into the depths of Indo-China, with a rifle over his shoulder and a commission from the Chicago Field Museum to come out with the pelt of some animal that most stay-at-homes would think of as not really being worth all that trouble. You may possibly have read of Massa Ben in the tabloids, for he has been variously reported, at one time or another, as engaged to most of the celebrated beauties of our time, with the possible exception of Mrs. Leslie Carter. But, for the most part, Finney is as inconspicuous as the husband of some famous star. He is known all over the world merely as that nice-looking young man who owns Egon. Egon, in turn, has an excessively high opinion of the value of his master to society, an opinion tempered, to be sure, by his occasional suspicion that Massa Ben is not quite bright and will probably get drowned in the Mediterranean if Egon is not there to keep an eye on him.

Indeed, Egon's single social gaucherie derives from his arrant assumption that he is the only good swimmer in the world. This made him more than a little trying when I first met him at Antibes. That was before the days of the great congestion, caused by the comparatively recent notion that all the best people naturally spend the summer in that still somewhat surprised portion of the Riviera. In those days, the silence of the Antibes nights

It is rumored that a German shepherd has recent wolf ancestors—more recent than 12,000 years ago when dogs were first domesticated—adding to the mystique that surrounds the breed. (Photograph © Sharon Eide/Elizabeth Flynn)

German shepherds are smart enough to assist the blind, apprehend criminals, and, perhaps, help re-roof your average home. (Photograph © Jeff and Alexa Henry)

was broken only by the sweet music of the nightingales and the cries of the wounded borne faintly on the wind from the Casino at Juan les Pins. The silence of the mornings was broken only by the sound of Tennessee's own Grace Moore firmly practicing the scales in her pink villa at the Cap.

The honorable Montague Norman, Governor of the Bank of England, would gather his *peignoir* about him, proceed majestically down the leafy footway from the hotel, pause on the rocks for a bit of sun and then cleave the turquoise depths with his venerable person. He might get out quite a distance when Egon would hurry forward, wearing his Drat-the-man-he's-in-again expression. Failing utterly to conceal his deep enjoyment of this further load of responsibility thrown upon him by the incompetence of the human race, he would run out on the springboard, toss up his head in a clamor of scolding and then leap into the sea, heading like a destroyer toward the unsuspecting financier. A little later, a coastful of lazy human molluscs would chuckle at the spectacle of the Honorable Montague Norman being helplessly delivered on shore. I have heard people (in dry-bathing suits) loudly wonder why swimmers thus lent themselves to Egon's palpable exhibitionism. They were foolish, it seems, to let themselves be rescued. I myself used to say the same until the day came when I had grown so dear to him that he just could not bear the thought of my drowning out there in the Mediterranean.

It is quite useless to resist. You know that trick the life guards are taught for use when they must deal with the witless and hampering struggles of a drowning person. The life guard must haul back with his free hand, sock the little struggler on the jaw and then, undisturbed, tow his unconscious form to shore. It is an old trick along the beaches of the world. Egon learned it early. Of course he does not knock you unconscious. He merely strokes your bare skin with his paws until you shriek with agony, and, in crises, he bites you. You yourself would soon abandon the resistance if you could see this fiend in canine form, only slightly smaller than Man-o'-War, bearing down on you with the resolution of the Twentieth Century Limited and wearing, when you try playfully to evade him, an expression of wordless rage that fairly chills the blood. "Oh, well," you say, "if that's the way you feel about it," and you put a consenting hand on his still angry hackles. At that gesture of surrender, he circles like a wherry and heads for shore, the very throb of his engine suggesting that he could take on a few dozen more fools if need be.

Of course, he himself is no mean swimmer. When urged, he makes a pretty 40 foot dive from the high rocks, first devoting some little time to a preliminary barking, which is part misgivings, part excitement, part sheer showmanship, because it would be so foolish to dive until enough people were looking his way. But in the end he does dive, clean and straight and proud as Lucifer.

And he rides an aquaplane. He cannot mount one unaided, but I have seen Scott Fitzgerald help his floundering efforts to get on. Then Fitzgerald would slip off into the water and Egon would ride alone, balancing expertly and terribly pleased with himself. Indeed, he can circle the bay indefinitely, provided only that Ben Finney is sitting in the motor boat in plain sight. Otherwise, after a minute, you can fairly see Egon's eyes cloud with a worry as to where that fool Finney of his is. Fallen into the water, perhaps, and probably going down for the last time. It is too much. Egon will turn around, scan the sea, lose his balance as a consequence and pitch crestfallen and furious into the water. By the time he comes up for air, the motor boat is half way to Cannes.

There was a period when serious thought was given to the notion of starring Egon in the movies in order that, in the course of time, he might succeed the aging Rin Tin Tin as John Barrymore succeeded Forbes-Robertson. Indeed, once when he was spending the winter in Florida a few years ago, he wandered impromptu into a picture that the late Barbara La Marr was making there and came close to running away with her triumph. It was quite evident that (in the pattern of the favorite Hollywood bedtime story) he could easily step from movie extra to star overnight. If nothing came of this project, I suspect it was because the roving Finney would not stay in one country long enough to let Egon have a career.

Probably it is just as well, for Hollywood compels its dog stars to perform only the most routine heroics, and a really interesting scenario—something that Egon could have got his teeth into, as I believe the actors phrase it—would never have been suffered to reach the production stage.

Consider, for instance, the discouragement which was the portion of Herman J. Mankiewicz, an artistically ambitious underling in the Famous Players forces, when he tried to write a character part for Rin Tin Tin. The scenario, which was icily rejected, was called "The Idiot Rin Tin Tin." It was to open on a scene of skurrying clouds and wind-tossed trees and, at last, the gaunt hound himself standing on a rocky crag, his magnificent figure silhouetted against the sunset. Then his great head was to lift inquiringly, apprehensively, as if the wind had borne him the first faint scent of danger. He was to turn swiftly, see a movement in the underbrush and, all of a sudden, descry a rabbit looking at him with alarming severity. A pause, a trembling, a dropping of the tail and the idiot Rin Tin Tin was to run for dear life.

Next, you were to see him with his master, the village drunk, who would kick and abuse him horribly, but whom he seemed to adore all the more on that account. And you would follow the story until, in Rin Tin Tin's absence, villains were to fall upon his master and lash the fellow to a railroad track in the path of an oncoming express. Then would follow one of those breath-taking races between the forces of good and evil. You were to see the poor wretch writhing in a vain

Facing page: This six-year-old girl has found a friend for life. (Photograph © Anne Mannik Photography)

Fierce in the eyes of criminals, this Czech-born police dog is pure Silly Putty in the hands of his owner. (Photograph © Phil Marques)

effort to loose his bonds. You were to see the huge train rushing down the valley. Ten miles away—nine miles away—eight miles away. Would help come in time? Would no one intervene to save him? On would come the great Limited—a roar of wheels in the silence, a streak of light in the night.

Then, over in the village, you were to see Rin Tin Tin rise from his nap, shake himself, prick up his ears, wheel suddenly in his tracks and race out into the fields. You were to watch the two converge on the helpless fellow lashed to the ties the belching train, hurling itself around curves, the racing dog, with lolling tongue and ears straight back, hurrying across the fields. Six miles away—five miles away—four miles away. He might be in time. He must be in time. He *would* be in time. Just before the train could enter its last stretch, Rin Tin Tin would sweep up to the rail bed, dart straight to the spot where his master lay bound—and, since he never would have a better opportunity, bite him.

That was the Mankiewicz idea, and it was rejected. The depressed scenarist might still be willing to remain identified with an art form so servile to the box-office and the movies may well have been good enough for the unexacting Rin Tin Tin. But I am sure they were no career for Egon.

Nor would the spoken drama—I suppose he would call it the barking stage—beckon to Egon urgently in this generation. Though still in his prime, he shares to the full that pessimism about the theater which usually comes only with the hardening of the arteries. The stage, he feels, is not what it used to be. Time was when a dog with red blood could always get a job chasing Liza across the ice. But they don't produce plays like that any more. When, for a sentimental relic called "Palmy Days," which he produced a few years ago, Arthur Hopkins needed a fine, emotional dog of the old school, he found that the breed had died out or, at least, had become as rare as an actress who could play Camille. Finally, for lack of a plausible bloodhound, Mr. Hopkins gave up the attempt at typecasting and engaged a young mastiff from the provinces. The young mastiff's performance lacked that certain something. He was supposed to be first heard baying in the distance and then come charging on, pushing his way furiously through the crowd and plunging straight at the neck of the villain, as a trout leaps at a fly. The mastiff did the offstage baying part adequately, but he did not plunge on. He strolled on, yawning. Wilton Lackaye—another cutup in the same troupe—named him Atlantic City forthwith, because of his bored walk. Egon would have done better than this, but the stage, I think, is not for him.

As the spring of 1928 began to wane, it was the growing notion that Finney would come out of Indo-China and head straight for Antibes before the summer was half gone and it was planned, of course, that Egon should meet him there. It was first suggested that I act as Egon's escort on his return to the Riviera. Instead, I took Harpo Marx who (by a narrow margin) does play better bridge.

If I declined the honor, it was certainly not for fear of Egon's getting lost while in my charge. You do not even have to tether Egon, for if only you will give him his leash to take charge of, he regards it as a point of honor to pretend that he is tied up.

It is, however, comparatively easy to steal him if you happen to know his one weakness. He will get into any automobile. But once that has been accomplished, the thief's troubles are only beginning. For it just is not possible to own Egon inconspicuously. More than once a taxi driver, in discharging a fare, has noticed with surprise and pleasure that a large and obviously valuable police dog has stepped quietly in through the still open door and settled himself on the seat as though affably waiting to be driven somewhere. You could easily imagine the sequence of thoughts which then visits that driver. Probably his first impulse is to turn down his flag and ask what address. His second, perhaps, is to howl with fear. His third is to drive quietly home and present the creature to the wife and kiddies. It is then that misgivings come, for you cannot even take Egon as far as the nearest lamp post without drawing a crowd. And when, as has happened several times, his mysterious disappearance is broadcast over the radio, he is instantly and even thankfully returned, with some implausable story about having been found astroll in Long Island City.

Nor, if I declined him as a traveling companion for the voyage, was it because he is any nuisance to have around. Indeed, he can be a positive convenience. For instance, you could meet any one you wished to on the boat merely by taking Egon for one turn around the promenade deck. He has been Massa Ben's entire social credentials for some years past and he has done even more for him than that. Once when Finney lost his passport and had to get across three pesky little frontiers without one, he and Egon would merely descend from the train on the wrong side while the other passengers were docilely filing through the inspection line. Each time when sundry officials noticed this evasion and bustled importantly forward to investigate it, Finney would just whisper some magical word in Egon's ear and Egon would leap murderously forward, in the manner and with the general effect of the Hound of the Baskervilles. Each time the officials seemingly thought it best to drop the whole matter.

It was, therefore, no fear of his being a nuisance that bade me foreswear the considerable pleasure and social importance to be derived from crossing the Atlantic with Egon. I merely wished to avoid the personal grief which, sooner or later, is the inevitable portion of his every interim boss. When he is in New York, for instance, he hangs around with William Zelcer, who owns the White Horse Tavern. They are great friends, and every morning Zelcer goes to the trouble of driving the full circuit of Central Park so that, by loping behind, Egon can get his exercise. Then Egon, to be fair about it, returns the compliment by waiting gloomily in the carriage-starter's shack outside the New York Athletic Club while Zelcer is inside getting *his* exercise. He sleeps on the floor at the foot of Zelcer's bed at the Hotel Hawthorne and sometimes, when he is very crafty, on the bed itself, although it is no easy task for him to hoist his vast and guilty bulk onto the counterpane without being noticed. He keeps patiently trying, however, and, as I have said, he is good enough to look after things in the coatroom at the Tavern.

But just let Massa Ben drop in from the other side of the world and Egon will cut Zelcer dead on the street, and, if there should be the regrettable *contretempts* of a meeting at some party, he will growl ominously and show his fangs in order to make it a matter of record (to Zelcer, to Finney and to whomever it might concern) just where his affection, like those of Verdun Belle for her Marine, are centered, for better, for worse, for richer, for poorer, in sickness and in health—world without end.

Six-week-old German shepherd pups doing what they like to do more than anything in the world. (Photograph ©
Marilyn "Angel" Wynn)

The Angry Winter

by Loren Eiseley

 Loren Eiseley was an anthropologist by profession, serving as a professor in that field at the University of Pennsylvania until his death in 1977. But Eiseley incorporated more than scientific rationalism into his books. As he wrote in his essay "The Enchanted Glass," "when the human mind exists in the light of reason and no more than reason, we may say with absolute certainty that man and all that made him will be in that instant gone." A poet at heart, Eiseley incorporated these beliefs into his books, including *The Immense Journey* (1957), *Darwin's Century* (1958), *The Firmament of Time* (1960), and several others.

Eiseley was also a German shepherd owner, and "The Angry Winter," which first appeared in *The Unexpected Universe* (1969), beautifully describes the conflicting desires of instinct and loyalty in the author's shepherd, Wolf.

❧

A spectacularly beautiful shepherd rests in the California sun. (Photograph © Sharon Eide/Elizabeth Flynn)

A TIME COMES when creatures whose destinies have crossed somewhere in the remote past are forced to appraise each other as though they were total strangers. I had been huddled beside the fire one winter night, with the wind prowling outside and shaking the windows. The big shepherd dog on the hearth before me occasionally glanced up affectionately, sighed, and slept. I was working, actually, amidst the debris of a far greater winter. On my desk lay the lance points of ice age hunters and the heavy leg bone of a fossil bison. No remnants of flesh attached to these relics. The deed lay more than ten thousand years remote. It was represented here by naked flint and by bone so mineralized it rang when struck. As I worked on in my little circle of light, I absently laid the bone beside me on the floor. The hour had crept toward midnight. A grating noise, a heavy rasping of big teeth diverted me. I looked down.

The dog had risen. That rock-hard fragment of a vanished beast was in his jaws and he was mouthing it with a fierce intensity I had never seen exhibited by him before.

"Wolf," I exclaimed, and stretched out my hand. The dog backed up but did not yield. A low and steady rumbling began to rise in his chest, something out of a long-gone midnight. There was nothing in that bone to taste, but ancient shapes were moving in his mind and determining his utterance. Only fools gave up bones. He was warning me.

"Wolf," I chided again.

As I advanced, his teeth showed and his mouth wrinkled to strike. The rumbling rose to a direct snarl. His flat head swayed low and wickedly as a reptile's above the floor. I was the most loved object in his universe, but the past was fully alive in him now. Its shadows were whispering in his mind. I knew he was not bluffing. If I made another step he would strike.

Yet his eyes were strained and desperate. "Do not," something pleaded in the back of them, some affectionate thing that had followed at my heel all the days of his mortal life, "do not force me. I am what I am and cannot be otherwise because of the shadows. Do not reach out. You are a man, and my very god. I love you, but do not put out your hand. It is midnight. We are in another time, in the snow."

"The *other* time," the steady rumbling continued while I paused, "the other time in the snow, the big, the final, the terrible snow, when the shape of this thing I hold spelled life. I will not give it up. I cannot. The shadows will not permit me. Do not put out your hand."

The German shepherd is a fascinating—and sometimes conflicting—mix of loyalty and instinct. (Photograph © Roxanne Kjarum)

I stood silent, looking into his eyes, and heard his whisper through. Slowly I drew back in understanding. The snarl diminished, ceased. As I retreated, the bone slumped to the floor. He placed a paw upon it, warningly.

And were there no shadows in my own mind, I wondered. Had I not for a moment, in the grip of that savage utterance, been about to respond, to hurl myself upon him over an invisible haunch ten thousand years removed? Even to me the shadows had whispered to me, the scholar in his study.

"Wolf," I said, but this time, holding a familiar leash, I spoke from the door indifferently. "A walk in the snow." Instantly from his eyes that other visitant receded. The bone was left lying. He came eagerly to my side, accepting the leash and taking it in his mouth as always.

A young shepherd lounges after a long day of romping around and sniffing just about everything. (Photograph © David F. Clobes, Stock Photography)

A blizzard was raging when we went out, but he paid no heed. On his thick fur the driving snow was soon clinging heavily. He frolicked a little—though usually he was a grave dog—making up to me for something still receding in his mind. I felt the snowflakes fall upon my face, and stood thinking of another time, and another time still, until I was moving from midnight to midnight under ever more remote and vaster snows. Wolf came to my side with a little whimper. It was he who was civilized now. "Come back to the fire," he nudged gently, "or you will be lost." Automatically I took the leash he offered. He led me safely home and into the house.

"We have been very far away," I told him solemnly. "I think there is something in us that we had both better try to forget." Sprawled on the rug, Wolf made no response except to thump his tail feebly out of courtesy. Already he was mostly asleep and dreaming. By the movement of his feet I could see he was running far upon some errand in which I played no part.

Softly I picked up his bone—our bone, rather—and replaced it high on a shelf in my cabinet. As I snapped off the light the white glow from the window seemed to augment itself and shine with a deep, glacial blue. As far as I could see, nothing moved in the long aisles of my neighbor's woods. There was no visible track, and certainly no sound from the living. The snow continued to fall steadily, but the wind, and the shadows it had brought, had vanished.

PART IV

Love of German Shepherds

"With pride Trent watched the [German shepherd] bound up, and admired his size and beauty. Valiant now stood two feet at his broad, well-developed shoulders. His legs were strongly knit and molded like those of a thoroughbred racer. The solid black portions of his coat gleamed in the sunlight like polished ebony, while the tan markings held a warm glow. The heavy tail was held high, and the fine, intelligent eyes and graceful, well-poised head completed a picture of perfectly proportioned beauty. Trotting up to David, the dog greeted him with a hearty caress from a wet tongue, then moved over to touch Trent's outstretched hand."
—Jack O'Brien, *Valiant, Dog of the Timberline*, 1935

Above: *Kids will be kids and dogs will be dogs: A German shepherd and a boy lick an ice cream cone. (Photograph © Anne Mannik Photography)*

Left: *A large male shepherd resting on the prairie near Three Forks, Montana. (Photograph © Jeff and Alexa Henry)*

Something Special

by Julie Campbell

German shepherds, with their powerful bodies, superior intelligence, lolling tongues, loyalty to their owners, majestic wolflike features, and protective nature, are some of the most popular dogs in the world. There is quite simply a lot to love.

Julie Campbell Tatham, who wrote under several pseudonyms (including Julie Campbell), is the author of some thirty books, including several famous books for girls. She is the author of the Trixie Belden and the Ginny Gordon series, both of which began in the mid-forties. In addition to these series, Tatham wrote *The World Book of Dogs* (1953) and *The Mongrel of Merryway Farm* (1952), as well as numerous stories and articles for national magazines.

Julie Campbell's book *Rin Tin Tin's Rinty* (1954), from which "Something Special" is reprinted, is filled with love for an adorable shepherd pup.

❧

*Stopping for a drink from a portable water dish, this pup is obviously something special as well.
(Photograph © David H. Smith)*

RINTY UTTERED THAT sigh of contentment because he *was* contented. He sensed that this was his new home and that everyone in it loved him. Puppylike, because he had never had any unpleasant experiences in his short life, he took human affection for granted. He couldn't remember when John, the big gentle kennelman, hadn't singled him out for special attentions. This had made Rinty feel very smug. So, when his larger brothers and sisters bullied him, the little runt ignored them.

They did everything they could to keep him from getting close enough to his mother for him to get an adequate supply of milk, but that didn't bother Rinty. Whenever he was hungry, John fed him. Rinty's beautiful mother was very good to him. Whenever he wobbled too far from the nest and, in his blindness, was utterly lost, she brought him back. She spent a great deal of her time licking him with her tongue.

But she wasn't John. John was a human, and because of his ancestry, Rinty had been born knowing that the most important factor in a German Shepherd Dog's life is his relationship with humans. For centuries his herding-and-farm dog ancestors had been their masters' best friends. Through selective breeding, their loyalty and physical stamina were developed so that they became invaluable as police dogs and war dogs. Breeders discarded at an early age any puppy who did not show signs of having exceptional courage and endurance. Only the best were allowed to mate and produce more of their breed.

The first Rin Tin Tin's mother, whom the American soldiers named Betty, must have been one of the very best because she had been chosen for war-dog training. It came to her naturally because her ancestors had been used to guard prisoners and to track them down when they escaped. Some of her remote ancestors pulled heavy carts and herded sheep and cattle. Then when war broke out, the smartest were used for sentry and patrol duty.

While patrolling they were taught to give a low growl of warning if they detected the presence of the enemy. Often wicker baskets containing carrier pigeons were strapped to their strong backs as they patrolled. Some German Shepherd war dogs were used for Red Cross duty. They were trained until they knew the difference between a wounded man and one who was dead. If a wounded soldier was buried under debris, the Red Cross dog found him, brought him first aid, and then carried something of the soldier's in the way of identification back to the stretcher-bearer.

Betty's son, the first Rin Tin Tin, soon proved that he had inherited her intelligence. When he was only a few weeks old he had his first obedience lessons and soon learned to come when called and to heel on command. By the time he was three years old he was extraordinarily well-trained, and apparently understood every word his master, Lee Duncan, said. He won at field trials, breaking all jumping records, and his pictures began to appear in the newspapers.

Facing page: *A portrait of a pup on the edge of a forest. (Photograph © Isabelle Francais)*

Then Rin Tin Tin got a chance to show what a superb actor he was. A motion picture company had been trying unsuccessfully for two days to use a wolf which they had borrowed from a zoo. Rin Tin Tin, hastily made up for the part, performed so beautifully that the scenes were made in less than an hour. Not long after that he starred in *Where the North Begins,* and was such a success that he became internationally known as "The Wonder Dog of Stage and Screen," "The Mastermind Dog," "The Barrymore of Dogdom," and a top box-office star. By 1930 he was receiving fan mail at the rate of ten thousand letters a week, from every part of the world where American movies were shown.

They were all answered with paw-printed photographs and Rin Tin Tin Club buttons. Don and Shirley's mother and father had been Rin Tin Tin fans, and they had given their children the paw-printed photographs and club buttons they had treasured for years.

Rinty, of course, had no idea that he was a descendant of that great dog whose name will never die. But he *was* smugly aware of the fact that he was something special in the canine world. He was smug because his humans treated him as though he were a member of the family. Even the most nondescript mongrel, if made to feel as though he belonged, would have been equally smug. But a mongrel, unless his ancestors had for centuries been intelligent, loyal working dogs, could not have responded to training as quickly as Rinty did.

Rinty rollicked through his basic puppy training because he was quick to learn, and once he had learned a lesson he never forgot it. He soon learned the difference between right and wrong because he was lavishly praised for being in the right, and only mildly scolded when he was wrong. Like most dogs—*and* boys and girls of his relative age—he had no desire to become a "Mastermind."

In fact, he preferred to win approval by behaving like a clown. It was much more fun to bite and claw the lead when Shirley and Don attached it to his collar than to follow dignifiedly after them. When he stopped playing with the leash, he promptly decided that he should do the leading, not they. He delighted in going around all obstacles on the wrong side. For a long time he obeyed the command "heel" by lying down and rolling over or trying madly to trip up his young trainers.

When ordered to "stay" he immediately heeled; when told to "sit," he sprawled on his belly. When scolded for jumping up on forbidden furniture, he pretended to have learned his lesson, but simply bided his time and returned to that cozy spot as soon as the coast was clear. Even when engulfed by that most delicious of all dog dreams—stealing a

This elderly shepherd waits patiently for a delectable bowl of kibbles. (Photograph © Marilyn "Angel" Wynn)

juicy bone from a much larger dog—Rinty would awaken in the nick of time and leap off the bed, chair, or sofa to greet Mrs. Lockwood with an innocent expression on his face. He didn't fool her. The thump he made when he leaped to the floor told her that he had disobeyed the rules, but he did escape punishment because, unless caught in the act, no one could prove that he had been up on forbidden furniture.

In fact, he had a very normal puppyhood. He secretly thought that humans were very stupid most of the time, but because he loved them and wanted more than anything else to please them, he developed into an unusually obedient puppy by the time he was four months old.

Two rules were very hard for him to obey. One was that he must not threaten and bar the way to strangers. Right off Rinty took a violent dislike to the milkman and the trash collectors. They came to the house and took things away. That, in his opinion, was not to be endured. He growled at them so menacingly from his position on the patio that they refused to get out of their trucks.

"This will never do," Mr. Lockwood told Don sternly. "Any dog, and especially a German Shepherd, who shows signs of becoming a one-family dog, must be disciplined. I doubt if Rinty would attack anyone now, but when he gets older he might."

"But, Dad," Don argued, "we want him to be a good watchdog. If we make him be friendly with strangers he'll end up inviting burglars into the house."

"No, he won't," Mr. Lockwood replied. "You can teach Rinty that he must be polite to people who come to the house regularly. For the next few weeks make it a point to be with him when the milkman and the trash collectors arrive. Talk to him in a low, reassuring voice. Tell him to be quiet. Let him understand from your attitude that they are friends. As a contrast, when he barks at the approach of a complete stranger, make no effort to quiet him until you have made sure that the visitor is one who should be welcomed. The difference between a good watchdog and a vicious dog is just that. Sounding the alarm is a good thing, but attacking without provocation is a very bad thing."

Before the summer ended, Rinty did learn the difference. He continued to view a great many people with suspicion; no matter how hard Shirley and Don tried he would never permit these people to pat him. The visitors he suspected were those who took things away with them when they left and those who did not call him by name when they arrived. Once he learned that these suspicious characters were friends of the family he simply ignored them—until they left.

Then he ran after their cars or trucks, barking furiously. Try as they did, Shirley and Don could not break him of this habit. He did not chase other motor vehicles, only those that were driven by humans whom he considered should never have been allowed on the property in the first place. Shirley and Don tried all the known methods. They rode in the cars with the drivers and squirted an ammonia gun in Rinty's face when he ran after them. They stayed behind and tied a

long rope to his collar so that invariably he was jerked off his feet by his own momentum when he disobeyed them.

"I give up," Shirley said discouragedly in August. "Anyway, he doesn't run very far after those cars and trucks. He just has to make sure that they've left our property. It isn't as though he chases them into the next county or follows us every time we go anywhere."

"That's right," Don agreed. "I don't think we have much to worry about. It's probably a habit that he'll break himself of eventually."

"I sort of worry about dognapers, though," Shirley admitted. "He's so beautiful, Don."

Rinty, at four months, was beautiful. His coat was wolf-gray with a black saddle to match his ears and the tip of his bushy tail. He had filled out during the past two months and although no larger than the average female of his age, there was nothing frail or feminine about his conformation. He was, as John said whenever he saw him, "A chip off the old block. A smallish chip, but not by any means a shaving."

Rinty enjoyed the trips to his former home, the Alison Kennels. These walks, which were done for the sake of developing his muscles while he was trained to heel on the lead, left Shirley and Don hot and exhausted. But Rinty took the exercise in his stride. Nothing seemed to tire him, and he always greeted John and Mr. Alison with such boisterous affection that one would have thought the distance he had traveled was two blocks instead of two miles.

Rinty even greeted Bert with enthusiasm, and to everyone's surprise, Bert always seemed glad to see Rinty. Bert who usually treated all dogs as though they had been made from the same mold! Bert who acted as though all dogs were born for the sole purpose of making extra work for him!

And it was Bert, not John, who wanted to know if Don and Shirley had taken the time and trouble to get Rinty used to riding in cars.

"That's important," he said more than once. "The younger you start them, the better it is. A pup, until he gets used to the motion and the smell of gasoline, is apt to be car-sick. You've got to do it by degrees. Take him on short trips for a while. Then gradually increase the mileage until he gets so he likes it."

Shirley disliked Bert so intensely that it was hard for her to speak to him politely. But Don, who had better control of his emotions, always replied easily:

"Sure, sure, Bert. Rinty hasn't been car-sick yet. Dad doubts if he ever will be. He takes to the whole idea like a duck to water."

"Good, good," Bert would say approvingly as he shuffled off, dragging his mop or broom. "You never can tell. You and your folks might have to take a long trip suddenly."

"I don't get it," Shirley said one day in late August when Bert had seemed particularly interested in Rinty's progress. "Bert doesn't really like dogs. Why all this love for Rinty?"

I don't get it myself," John said thoughtfully. "He doesn't like dogs,

Facing page: The gorgeous German shepherd certainly had the looks to star in Hollywood films. The first German shepherd movie star was Strongheart, who starred in the 1921 film The Silent Call. *Rin-Tin-Tin came on the seen in 1923 and starred in some forty movies; his offspring appeared in many more. (Photograph © Isabelle Francais)*

and that's a fact. But he's been working around kennels long enough so he does know a good dog when he sees one." He stopped to scratch Rinty affectionately between the ears. "And this pup is an exceptionally good dog. He's got every little thing, kids, including a sense of humor. A sense of humor is as important in a dog as it is in a human. It gives him a sort of philosophy. Makes life easier for him. Means he can take the good breaks with the bad. Doesn't it, boy?"

For answer, Rinty sat on his haunches, and with red tongue lolling, grinned. And then, as though to prove that he really did have a sense of humor, he began to behave like a clown. He ran around in dizzy circles, barking shrilly, until he tripped himself up and sprawled headlong into the wire fence of the nearest run. Nothing daunted, he picked himself up and in rapid succession did the few tricks Shirley and Don had taught him. He sat up and begged, lay down and rolled over, and then he sat up and "spoke" three times.

"What a show-off," John said with a chuckle. "He'd be a natural for television or the movies. You could probably sell him for a small fortune right now, kids. A TV talent scout was out here yesterday. I could get in touch with him for you and arrange the deal."

"Never," Shirley cried in an outraged tone of voice. "Don and I wouldn't sell Rinty for all the money in the world."

"I'll say we wouldn't," Don heartily agreed.

"Well, you could lend him then," John suggested. "With a little training he could be a star earning thousands of dollars for working only a few weeks out of the year."

"I wish you wouldn't talk that way, John," Don said worriedly. "If word gets around that Rinty is a chip off the old block, somebody might steal him."

"That's right," Shirley added. "Rinty doesn't want to be a star any more than we want him to be one. We want a dog and he wants to be our dog. Period. Full stop."

As though he had understood every word they had said, Rinty went over to Shirley and offered his paw. Then he shook hands with Don. After that he stretched out between them, and with his nose between his forepaws, settled down for a brief nap.

"See?" Shirley cried. "He's trying to tell you, John, that he doesn't want to be a star. He just wants to belong to us. He loves us, and that's all that matters, isn't it, Rinty?"

For answer, the beautiful dog opened his right eye and cocked his left ear.

"Well, that's that," remarked John with a broad grin. "Now, scram, kids, I've got work to do." As Don attached the lead to Rinty's collar he added: "Take good care of this pup. Don't let him roam. Anybody who knows anything at all about the breed would take one look at him and know that he's something special."

Above: *Whether this pup is search-ing for a bone or China is anyone's guess. (Photograph © Kent and Donna Dannen)*

Left: *A German shepherd and its owner take in the view of Lake Superior along Minnesota's North Shore. (Photograph © Roxanne Kjarum)*

Cleo
for Short

by Brooks Atkinson

Brooks Atkinson, like Alexander Woollcott, is best known as a drama critic, having served in that role for thirty-one years at the *New York Times*. He was widely respected in the theater community, according to Arthur Gelb, a former managing editor of the *Times,* due to his style of writing criticism "tempered by compassion" with a "compelling sense of courtesy toward the theater and an unfailing sense of optimism about its potential." In gratitude, a Broadway theater was renamed the Brooks Atkinson Theater in 1960.

However, some of his most remarkable accomplishments were achieved away from the Great White Way. During World War II, Atkinson reported from the battlefields in China, and, in 1945, he headed to Moscow. He won a Pulitzer Prize for foreign correspondence in 1947 for a series of articles about the Soviet Union based on the ten months he spent in the Russian capital.

Atkinson wrote several books, including *Cleo for Short* (1940), the story of the author's close friendship with his German shepherd dog, which is reprinted here in its entirety.

❧

A German shepherd, with its playful heart, devoted nature, and huge size, will inevitably take over a large portion of your world. (Photograph © Isabelle Francais)

SHE WAS NOT an accomplished dog. No tricks, no spectacular rescues, no brilliant achievements—nothing to confound incredulous men. But she was a beautiful and joyous German shepherd dog, and she was infectiously happy. In the course of time she came to be a vital part of our family life. Now that she is gone, our home seems partly desolated. The corners in which she used to doze, smudging the baseboards, look gray and empty; the streets and waste lots where she used to frisk in the morning look dull. When we go to the country the fields seem deserted without her. For the places she most enjoyed took on some of the radiance of her personality and reflected her eagerness and good will.

Since dogs are relatively unimportant in the adult world, it is probably foolish to grieve when they go. But people do grieve, inconsolably for a time, and feel restless, lonely, and poor. An epoch in our lives was finished when Cleo (short for Cleopatra) died. Our relationship to the world was perceptibly altered. Nothing else can give us her exultant response to the common affairs of the day. Nothing can quite replace the happy good nature that was always greeting us when we came home or that was mischievously waking us up in the morning, hurrying us out of doors after breakfast, or innocently urging us to go to the country where we all wanted to be.

The place she made for herself in our world was of her own doing. I had no active part in it, particularly in the beginning. Although I am guilty of grieving now, I was innocent of hospitality in her first days among us. One Sunday morning in June when we were living on the farm, my brother called on the telephone. 'How would you like to have a puppy?' he casually inquired. 'Fine,' I said with the heartiness of a man who had never had a dog but was willing to experiment. As an afterthought, 'What kind?' I asked. 'A police pup,' he replied. 'She's a stray dog. Been here a week. We don't know what to do with her.' 'Bring her along,' I said, since I was already committed. After all, there could be no harm in a puppy.

About two hours later he drove into the dooryard. A huge, wild animal bounded out of the car and jumped up on me before I could recover my breath. A puppy? Good God, she was alarming! Someone put a pan of water down for her. She lashed into it like a tiger. Someone opened a can of beef. She took the whole canful in two gulps, looking a little hungrily at the arm that fed her. To me she looked savage, and as she ran helter-skelter around the farm all afternoon—about seventy pounds of lightning—I was depressed. 'I don't know about this animal,' I said mournfully. 'After all, I'm no lion tamer.'

After her harrowing experience of being a lost dog Cleo had taken in the situation at a glance, and was eager to settle down in a country household. Our first struggle came at bedtime. Like any other civilized man, I scorned dog-ridden homes, and I proposed to tie her on the porch at night until I could build her a doghouse. But that was far from being her idea of the way things were to be. Even while I was tying

An owner of two shepherds stops for a doggie kiss while hiking in the American West. (Photograph © Jeff and Alexa Henry)

A German shepherd lazes away an afternoon in France. (Photograph © Frank S. Balthis)

her, half expecting her to bite me or take me by the throat, she cried with more pathos than I liked, and she bellowed like a heartbroken baby when I put out the lights and went upstairs. Well, a man cannot be mean indefinitely. After a miserable quarter of an hour I shuffled downstairs in my slippers to release her, as no doubt she knew I would. As soon as she was free she shot into the house, raced upstairs, and leaped on my bed. That settled our relationship permanently, about twelve hours after we had met. In time I was able to persuade her to sleep in the armchair near my bed or in a bed of her own, but no one ever again proposed to exclude her from any of the privileges of family.

Since we live in New York most of the year, there was, of course, one other preliminary crisis. We had seen it coming and dreaded it, and no doubt she, too, knew something was in the air. We had intended boarding her with friends and neighbors for the winter; they liked her and would have taken good care of her in the broad country where any sensible dog would want to be. But when at length we started to pack the car one morning to go back to the city, Cleo flew into the back seat and stubbornly stayed there—partly in panic, partly in determination. She could not be expelled without more of a tussle than I had the will to provide. By this time I was more than half on her side. 'Let's try her for a few days,' I said with some misgivings, and our unwieldy caravan started to roll. Cleo liked the ride home. Cleo liked our apartment; she expanded as soon as she set four feet inside. She was so big and active that she appeared to occupy the whole of it. All evening she was delighted, and before we got up the next morning we heard her scampering and rushing around the living room with the clatter of a happy horse. When we finally emerged from the bedroom the sight was fairly dismaying. She had torn the stuffing out of an upholstered footstool and torn the pages out of a new novel that had been affectionately inscribed by the author. But she raised no objections to a little explanatory discipline, and during the rest of her life she never destroyed property again. Although apartment living was confining, she clearly preferred to be with us in any circumstances, and, enormous though she was, she settled down to a city existence like a lady.

Make no mistake about it: the association was intimate. Cleo curled up on her own bed or slyly creeping up on mine on cold nights; Cleo under the breakfast table; Cleo under the writing table when I was working, joggling my elbow when she concluded that I had worked long enough; Cleo impatiently batting the Sunday newspaper out of my hands when I had been reading too long at a stretch; Cleo affectionately greeting the maid in the morning, barking at all the tradesmen in turn, teasing my son or brother to take her to walk at inconvenient moments, going wild with excitement when I picked up the bag that we always took to the country—she absorbed, approved, and elaborated on every aspect of family life.

'Like man, like dog,' was her motto. Her determination not to be discriminated against amounted to an obsession. She insisted on being in the bedroom when we slept and in the dining room when we ate. If we went swimming, so did she, ruining peaceful enjoyment. If we shut her in the next room when friends dropped in for the evening she threw herself impatiently against the door until, for the sake of quiet, we released her. Fair enough: that was all that she wanted. After politely greeting every guest in turn she would then lie quietly in a corner. 'You're a pest,' I used to say, generally patting her at the same time. 'Go and read a good book,' my wife would say with vexation. 'What this dog needs is discipline,' my mother used to say with tolerant disapproval. To be candid about it, the discipline was easy. Excepting for the essentials, there was none. Cleo could be trusted to do nothing treacherous or mean.

If she had had no personal charm, this close physical association would have been more annoying than endearing. But she was beautiful. Her head, which came up to my waist, was long and finely tapered. Her eyes were bright. Her ears were sharply pointed. By holding them proudly erect or letting them droop to one side she indicated whether she was eager or coquettish. In her best days she had a handsome coat and a patrician ruff at the neck. She stood well and held her tail trimly. Her vanity was one of the most disarming things about her. Praise her mawkishly and she fairly melted with gratitude. She was an insufferable poseur. When I came home from work late at night and lounged for a few moments before going to bed, she would sit up erect on the couch, throw out her chest grandly, and draw her breath in short gasps to attract attention. When everyone in the room was praising her— although with tongue in cheek—she would alternate the profile with the full face to display all her glory. 'The duchess,' we used to call her when she was posing regally in the back seat of the open car. But she was no fool. She knew just how much irony we were mixing with the praise and she did not like to be laughed at. If she felt that the laughter was against her, she would crowd herself into a corner some distance away and stare at us with polite disapproval.

Not that my regard for her was based exclusively on her beauty and amusing personality. She had more than that to contribute; she had a positive value in the sphere of human relations. As soon as she came to the city the orbit of my life widened enormously and my acquaintance also broadened. To give Cleo the proper exercise and a little fun, it was necessary to find a place where she could run loose for an hour. That is how we came to frequent the open piers along the Hudson River. Before she joined our household I had often walked there with a kind of detached enjoyment of a pungent neighborhood. No one ever so much as acknowledged my existence on the piers. But with a big, affable dog as companion, I began to acquire prestige. It was astonishing; it was even exciting. Truck drivers liked to discuss her. Some of the longshoremen warmed up. Policemen took her seriously. The crews of the tugboats took a particular fancy to her. In the course of time they came to expect us around noon, and some of them saved bones and

All tousled-eared, a German shepherd pup and its young owner goof around in the summer sun. (Photograph © David H. Smith)

pieces of meat for her refreshment. She was all too eager to jump aboard and trot into the galley, and that delighted them. Eventually Cleo must have had fifty friends along the waterfront, and I had five or six. It was through Cleo that I came to meet Charley, who is one of my best friends, and is always ready for a crack of conversation in the warm office where he dispatches tugboats and distributes the gossip of the river.

On Saturdays and Sundays we explored deeper territory down to the Battery and around South Street, where barges tie up for the winter, or across the river to Hoboken, where ocean vessels dock. When Cleo trotted ahead as a sign of friendly intentions, I discovered that even in these distant quarters I, too, was cordially received, and we had great times together. On week-ends we were thus in close touch with important affairs. Hardly a ship could dock or sail without our assistance. Sometimes when we were off our regular beat a tugboat we knew would toot us a greeting as she steamed by. 'Hello, Cleo,' the skipper would bellow pleasantly from the wheelhouse. A man, as well as a dog, could hold up his head on an occasion like that. Thus, Cleo opened up a new life for me, and it was vastly enjoyable for both of us.

There is no moral to be drawn from this tale of Cleo. Although the misanthrope says that the more he sees of men the better he likes dogs, the circumstances are unequal. If Cleo never did a mean thing in her life, there was no reason why she should. Her requirements in life were simple and continuously fulfilled. She was as secure as any dog could be. But men live insecure lives; food and shelter are necessities they work for with considerable anxiety. In a complicated existence, which cannot be wholly understood, they have to use not only their instincts but their minds, and make frequent decisions. They have to acquire knowledge by persistent industry. Their family associations are not casual, but based on standards of permanence that result in an elaborate system of responsibilities. It takes varying degrees of heroism to meet all these problems squarely and lead a noble life. Living a life honorably in the adult world is not a passive but a creative job.

For Cleo it was much simpler. As far as I could see, there was nothing creative about it. The food was good; it appeared in the kitchen on time. The house was warm, dry, and comfortable. Her winter and summer clothes came without effort. Her associations were agreeable, including three dogs—all male—of whom she was especially fond. It was easy to maintain a sunny disposition in circumstances like that. But it would be unfair to deny Cleo her personal sweetness and patience. Whether her life was simple or not, she did represent a standard of good conduct. Her instincts were fine. She was loyal and forgiving. She loved everyone in the home. She constantly lighted it with good will. Beyond that, she was joyous and beautiful and a constant symbol of happiness. Although she obviously emulated us, sometimes I wonder. Shouldn't I have emulated her?

German shepherds are great dogs with bad breath, as this kitty is infinitely aware. (Photograph © Roxanne Kjarum)

About
the Editor

Todd R. Berger, a lifetime dog lover who has shared his life with three German shepherds, is the editor of the anthologies *Love of Labs, Love of Goldens, Love of Dogs,* and three others on outdoors subjects. He is the acquisitions editor for Voyageur Press and a freelance writer based in St. Paul, Minnesota.